P9-DHK-105

The Harlem Renaissance

Lucent Library of Black History

Andy Koopmans

LUCENT BOOKS

An imprint of Thomson Gale, a part of The Thomson Corporation

THOMSON

GALE

Detroit • New York • San Francisco • San Diego • New Haven, Conn.
Waterville, Maine • London • Munich

FRANKLIN SQ. PUBLIC LIBRARY
19 LINCOLN ROAD
FRANKLIN SQUARE, N.Y 11010

© 2006 Thomson Gale, a part of The Thomson Corporation.

Thomson and Star Logo are trademarks and Gale and Lucent Books are registered trademarks used herein under license.

For more information, contact
Lucent Books
27500 Drake Rd.
Farmington Hills, MI 48331-3535
Or you can visit our Internet site at http://www.gale.com

ALL RIGHTS RESERVED.
No part of this work covered by the copyright hereon may be reproduced or used in any form or by any means—graphic, electronic, or mechanical, including photocopying, recording, taping, Web distribution or information storage retrieval systems—without the written permission of the publisher.

Every effort has been made to trace the owners of copyrighted material.

LIBRARY OF CONGRESS CATALOGING-IN-PUBLICATION DATA

Koopmans, Andy.
   The Harlem Renaissance / by Andy Koopmans.
      p. cm. — (Lucent library of Black history)
   Includes bibliographical references and index.
   ISBN 1-59018-702-4 (hardcover : alk. paper)
   1. African Americans—Intellectual life—20th century—Juvenile literature. 2. Harlem Renaissance—Juvenile literature. 3. African Americans—History—1877-1964—Juvenile literature. 4. African American arts—History—20th century—Juvenile literature. 5. Harlem (New York, N.Y.)—Intellectual life—20th century—Juvenile literature. 6. New York (N.Y.)—Intellectual life—20th century—Juvenile literature. 7. African Americans—New York (State)—New York—Biography—Juvenile literature. I. Title. II. Series.
   E185.6.K66 2005
   974.7'100496073—dc22
                                                          2005000027

Printed in the United States of America

Contents

Foreword

It has been more than five hundred years since Africans were first brought to the New World in shackles, and over 140 years since slavery was formally abolished in the United States. Over 50 years have passed since the fallacy of "separate but equal" was obliterated in the American courts, and some forty years since the watershed Civil Rights Act of 1965 guaranteed the rights and liberties of all Americans, especially those of color. Over time, these changes have become celebrated landmarks in American history. In the twenty-first century, African American men and women are politicians, judges, diplomats, professors, deans, doctors, artists, athletes, business owners, and home owners. For many, the scars of the past have melted away in the opportunities that have been found in contemporary society. Observers such as Peter N. Kirsanow, who sits on the U.S. Commission of Civil Rights, point to these accomplishments and conclude, "The growing black middle class may be viewed as proof that most of the civil rights battles have been won."

In spite of these legal victories, however, prejudice and inequality have persisted in American society. In 2003, African Americans comprised just 12 percent of the nation's population, yet accounted for 44 percent of its prison inmates and 24 percent of its poor. Racially motivated hate crimes continue to appear on the pages of major newspapers in many American cities. Furthermore, many African Americans still experience either overt or muted racism in their daily lives. A 1996 study undertaken by Professor Nancy Krieger of the Harvard School of Public Health, for example, found that 80 percent of the African American participants reported having experienced racial discrimination in one or more settings, including at work or school, applying for housing and medical care, from the police or in the courts, and on the street or in a public setting.

It is for these reasons that many believe the struggle for racial equality and justice is far from over. These episodes of discrimi-

4

nation threaten to shatter the illusion that America has completely overcome its racist past, causing many black Americans to become increasingly frustrated and confused. Scholar and writer Ellis Cose has described this splintered state in the following way: "I have done everything I was supposed to do. I have stayed out of trouble with the law, gone to the right schools, and worked myself nearly to death. What more do they want? Why in God's name won't they accept me as a full human being?" For Cose and others, the struggle for equality and justice has yet to be fully achieved.

In many subtle yet important ways, the traumatic experiences of slavery and segregation continue to inform the way race is discussed and experienced in the twenty-first century. Indeed, it is possible that America will always grapple with the fallout from its distressing past. Ulric Haynes, dean of the Hofstra University School of Business has said, "Perhaps race will always matter, given the historical circumstances under which we came to this country." But studying this past and understanding how it contributes to present-day dialogues about race and history in America is a critical component of contemporary education. To this end, the Lucent Library of Black History offers a thorough look at the experiences that have shaped the black community and the American people as a whole. Annotated bibliographies provide readers with ideas for further research, while fully documented primary and secondary source quotations enhance the text. Each book in the series explores a different episode of black history; together they provide students with a wealth of information as well as launching points for further study and discussion.

Harlem, City of Hope

During the early decades of the twentieth century, African Americans faced enormous challenges. The rights and civil liberties that had been granted to them at the end of the Civil War had been under almost continuous assault. Segregation, limits on voting rights, and racist attacks combined so that for many blacks, life during this period was little better than it had been under slavery.

Harlem, and the flowering of African American culture that took place there, served as a bulwark against this tide of racism. Harlem was a place of hope in a difficult time. Moreover, the political and cultural ferment centered there filled many blacks throughout America with a sense that better times lay ahead.

The Renaissance Era in Harlem

Historians disagree on exactly when the flowering of African American culture known as the Harlem Renaissance began and ended. Some say it started in 1917, near the end of World War I, when black soldiers returning from Europe refused to resume being second-class citizens and began to demand the rights they had fought to protect in foreign lands. Others say the Harlem Renaissance dates from 1919, the year when massive race riots across the country raised awareness among other Americans of the many problems blacks faced. Still others mark its beginning as 1925, when the bulk of artistic activity actually began in Harlem itself.

Likewise, scholars debate the end of the Harlem Renaissance. Some say it ended with the stock market crash in October 1929, which helped bring on the Great Depression that in turn left few Americans with the money to support the arts. Others mark the end as March 1935, when a large race riot in Harlem damaged the area's image and ended the hope for better race relations that had existed among the many artists and writers who had created the Harlem Renaissance. Regardless of this uncertainty regarding its beginning and end, scholars agree that the Harlem Renaissance was the first time that African American literature, art, and music crossed racial lines to be accepted by large numbers of white Americans.

The Great Migration

There is, however, no debate over how this cultural flowering came to be centered in Harlem. Like many northern cities, New York was the terminus of a great migration of African Americans leaving the rural South. This movement from south to north had begun in the 1890s but greatly swelled in 1915 and continued at high levels through the 1920s. As a result, between 1890 and 1920, the black population of Manhattan rose from about 20,000 to over 109,000. That number doubled again by 1930.

A number of factors contributed to the great northward migration, including

Harlem

Four Outer Boroughs of New York City

Manhattan

New York

New Jersey

Bronx

Harlem

Manhattan

Queens

Brooklyn

Staten Island

Atlantic Ocean

economic depression in the South, the destruction of cotton crops by the boll weevil and by floods, the shortage of labor in the North caused by immigration restrictions and the demand for military recruits during World War I, and wages that were as much as three times higher in the North than they were in southern states. Furthermore, segregation and the persistent threat of violence at the hands of whites drove thousands of blacks north. However, according to Harlem Renaissance intellectual Alain Locke, beneath the economic and social reasons for the migration, there was a more fundamental and important motive: the hope for freedom of a sort that the South could not offer:

> The tide of Negro migration, northward and city-ward, is not to be fully explained as a blind flood started by the demands of war industry coupled with the shutting off of foreign migration, or by the pressure of poor crops coupled with increased social terrorism. . . . Neither labor demand-

During the Civil War, a family of fugitive slaves crosses a river as they flee northwards. After the war, thousands of freed slaves migrated north, many settling in New York.

ed [in the North], the boll weevil nor the Ku Klux Klan is a basic factor, however contributory any or all of them may have been. The wash and rush of this human tide on the beach line of the northern city centers is to be explained primarily in terms of a new vision of opportunity, of social and economic freedom, of a spirit to seize, even in the face of an extortionate and heavy toll, a chance for the improvement of conditions. With each successive wave of it, the movement of the Negro becomes more and more a mass movement toward the larger and the more democratic chance.[1]

Black Americans, then, looked to the North as a symbol of change, and few northern cities offered more hope than New York and its section known as Harlem.

Ascent of Harlem

As the first African Americans were moving to New York City, Harlem would have seemed an unlikely destination for them. In fact, these first immigrants settled in the lower Manhattan neighborhoods known as the Tenderloin and San Juan Hill. Over time, these neighborhoods became the most densely populated areas of the city and turned into slums rife with crime.

The Upper Manhattan neighborhood originally known as Haarlem had been a Dutch settlement; in the nineteenth century it had become an enclave of German, Jewish, and Irish working-class immigrants. It was not until the first decade of the twentieth century that the first blacks moved into Harlem. The first African American residence in the neighborhood was an apartment house on West 133rd Street. In 1905 a murder had been committed in one of the apartments there, and as a result the landlord found himself unable to attract any tenants. However, the building's owner employed a black real estate agent, Philip A. Payton, to find African American tenants who, because of the shortage of housing elsewhere, were willing to overlook the building's unfortunate history. In a short time, Payton had filled the building with black tenants. It was customary at the time for landlords to charge black tenants approximately $5 a month more in rent than they charged whites; again, because housing was in short supply, blacks had little choice but to pay the premium. The news of the higher profit to be gained from black tenants soon spread, and many other building owners in Harlem pushed their white tenants out and courted African Americans to move in. A massive immigration of blacks into Harlem began.

This influx of African Americans into what was a primarily white neighborhood angered and scared many of the original residents, who took action to keep the black renters out. However, these efforts were largely unsuccessful. Streets and then blocks and then groups of city blocks became inhabited entirely by African Americans. In 1914 Harlem's black neighborhood covered more than twenty square blocks. By 1920, the neighborhood had nearly tripled in size, running from 130th Street to 145th Street, and from Madison Avenue to Eighth Avenue.

Though few blacks owned property or businesses in Harlem, the neighborhood's culture changed. As historian Steven Watson writes, "Despite the paucity [scarcity] of economic ownership, Harlem had developed . . . the significant mass of residents necessary to forge an African-American identity."[2]

By the 1920s, then, Harlem was the most densely populated African American community in the country. A 1921 article in the *New York Dispatch* praised the thriving settlement:

> Fifteen years ago, Colored Harlem was confined to one or two city blocks. Today, Harlem's Colored People proudly claim almost the entire area north of 128th to 148th streets, from Park to Eighth avenues, a city . . . within a city. About two miles long by two miles wide, having more people than the entire combined population, whites and blacks, of Richmond and Lynchburg, Va., together. Here thrive many enterprises . . . large public schools, library, Y.M.C.A. and Y.W.C.A. buildings, casinos, theaters, political, social and music club houses; fraternal homes.[3]

To serve the growing African American population, black churches were built and businesses such as barbershops and bars opened. Civil rights organizations moved their headquarters into the neighborhood, drawing politically active African Americans. Cabarets in the neighborhood grew in number, and the entertainers who worked in these establishments soon followed.

This 1922 photo of a bustling street in Harlem gives some idea of how densely populated this neighborhood was in the 1920s.

Fostering Cooperation

Against this backdrop of migration, black intellectuals and civil rights leaders made a critical strategic decision. Taking note of an increased interest in black culture among many whites following World War I, thinkers such as W.E.B. DuBois saw an opportunity to foster interracial cooperation and understanding through the media of literature, visual arts, music, theater, and dance.

At the very least, these black leaders succeeded in fostering enormous artistic productivity. Out of this period of burgeoning creativity came twenty-six novels, ten volumes of poetry, five Broadway plays, many essays and short stories, several ballets and concertos, and a large number of paintings and sculptures, all created by African Americans. In addition, African American musicians and other performing artists reached large audiences, both black and white. In the process of reaching across previously impermeable racial boundaries, the artists of the Harlem Renaissance left for future generations of artists and civil rights activists a legacy that changed not only African American life but the face of American culture itself.

Chapter One

The "New Negro" Movement

The blossoming of literary and artistic activity known as the Harlem Renaissance would have been impossible had it not been for a period of heightened African American civil rights activism that arose during the early decades of the twentieth century. Led by intellectuals such as W.E.B. DuBois, the activists were collectively known as the "New Negro" movement. In their writings, these activists eloquently depicted the plight of black Americans.

The activism of the New Negro movement was in response to violence by white racists, wholesale discrimination, and legal manipulations that had, for half a century or more, prevented most African Americans from benefiting from the civil rights they had been granted following the Civil War. In fact, so restricted were most blacks in what they were allowed to do that freedom was barely distinguishable from slavery.

Eroding Civil Rights and Safety

The restrictions on their freedom were not what many African Americans had expected during the period of Reconstruction that followed the Civil War. Between 1865 and 1877, the federal government had acted to abolish slavery once and for all and to grant to black Americans the same rights enjoyed by whites by passing the Thirteenth, Fourteenth, and Fifteenth Amendments to the U.S. Constitution, as well as the Civil Rights Act of 1875. In fact, during Reconstruction blacks had made substantial political and social gains. Backed by the presence of federal troops, blacks in the South were able to vote, and a few won election to state legislatures and to Congress. However, Reconstruction ended in 1877 when federal troops were withdrawn. Southern whites quickly reimposed a segregated society in which blacks were never equal.

In the latter part of the nineteenth century the nation turned its attention to interests other than African American civil rights. The federal government's power to enforce those rights was severely limited as the U.S. Supreme Court interpreted the Constitution narrowly and overturned much civil rights legislation. The result was widespread discrimination—sometimes legally sanctioned, as in the Jim Crow laws in the South, and sometimes simply as a matter of common practice, as in the North.

Southern blacks had to contend not only with discrimination and segregation but with the imminent danger of violence. At its most extreme, this violence took the form of lynching, which was the mostly spontaneous public murder of an individual accused of a crime, often on flimsy or nonexistent evidence. In the last decades of the nineteenth century and the early years of the twentieth

W.E.B. DuBois was perhaps the most prominent black intellectual in early twentieth-century America.

A lynch mob in Louisiana disperses after hanging a black man accused of murdering a white man in 1938.

century, lynching in the southern and border states became almost an institution. It was the favored method by which whites terrorized blacks and maintained white supremacy. The victim of a lynching, then, might well be an African American whose only offense had been to challenge in some way—real or imagined—the status quo.

A New Politics

In the face of attacks on their civil rights, some blacks had even resigned themselves to second-class citizenship. For example, educator Booker T. Washington, who toward the end of the nine-teenth century had become the country's most prominent black leader, subscribed to the view that blacks should satisfy themselves with life within the bounds of segregation and not push for voting rights (which were denied to most blacks in the South). He argued that by displaying virtues like thrift, industry, and Christian morality, blacks would eventually earn the respect of whites, who would in turn respect their constitutional rights.

Washington's accommodationist stance found favor with whites and at first with many blacks. Eventually, however, opposition to Washington and his position grew. In the early 1900s many younger African Americans decided that putting up with discrimination, segregation, and violence was not going to gain them acceptance among whites nor increase their opportunities to exercise their civil rights.

The Color Line

Among Washington's most vocal critics was a scholar named W.E.B. DuBois, who, along with a number of other politically active blacks, had founded the National Association for the Advancement of Colored People (NAACP). DuBois and his fellow activists argued that accommodating segregation and racism while hoping for better days was fruitless.

Booker T. Washington, a prominent black intellectual, urged blacks to accept their inferior status until they could gain the respect of whites.

In 1903 DuBois published his first book, a collection of essays called *The Souls of Black Folk*, in which he discussed the importance of race in the new century's development. "The problem of the Twentieth Century is the problem of the color line," he wrote. He also wrote that, despite nearly a half-century of freedom, most blacks remained poorly educated and stuck in poverty:

For this much all men know: despite compromise, war, and struggle, the Negro is not free. . . . In the most cultured sections and cities of the South the Negroes are a segregated, servile caste,

Racism in Popular Culture and Science

■

In addition to Jim Crow laws, racial violence, and discrimination, in the 1910s and 1920s white racism was strengthened by both science and popular culture, including the release of the controversial film *Birth of a Nation*. Scholar Arnold Rampersad discusses this in his essay "Racial Doubt and Racial Shame in the Harlem Renaissance" (in Fabre and Feith's *Temples for Tomorrow*).

If their own renaissance began in 1917 . . . it might also be said that about the same time, white racism had its own sort of triumphant rebirth with the premiere in 1915 of D.W. Griffith's motion picture *Birth of a Nation*, based on Thomas Dixon's immensely successful anti-Black novel *The Clansman* (1905). The movie . . . helped to make possible the renaissance of the Ku Klux Klan, when an Atlanta preacher, Joseph Simmons, revived the organization not simply as a weapon against blackS but to "maintain Anglo Saxon civilization on the American continent from submergence due to the encroachment and invasion of alien people of whatever clime and color."

Supporting this rebirth around 1915 was the preponderant weight of contemporary scientific opinion on race. . . . [Social scientist] William McDougall of Harvard, for exam-

with restricted rights and privileges. . . . And the result of all this is, and in nature must have been, lawlessness and crime.[4]

The Souls of Black Folk became a widely read and highly influential book among many black intellectuals, including Claude McKay, who would gain renown as a writer during the Harlem Renaissance. "The book shook me like an earthquake,"[5] McKay later recalled.

The Crisis
The idea that accommodation would never work was further spread by the NAACP's official publication, the *Crisis*, which DuBois

ple, . . . warned of the grave perils of race intermingling. . . . No less an authority than the president of the American Sociological Society, Henry Pratt Fairchild, a professor of sociology at New York University, declared, "The principle has been propounded and urged by certain broadminded and sympathetic persons that there should be no racial discrimination in any American legislation. Nothing could be more unsound, unscientific, and dangerous. Racial discrimination is inherent in biological fact and in human nature. It is unsafe and fallacious to deny in legislation forces which exist in fact."

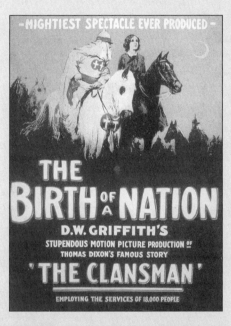

D.W. Griffith's controversial 1915 film *Birth of a Nation* romanticized the image of the Ku Klux Klan as the saviors of the white race.

edited and wrote for. In addition to advocating the end of racial discrimination in the journal's pages, he helped promote other causes, such as woman suffrage. The journal became known for its radical and confrontational positions against racism, prejudice, and violence.

Among the ideas the *Crisis* supported was Pan-Africanism, which emphasized the importance of unity and kinship among all people of African ancestry around the world. Those who advocated Pan-Africanism encouraged American blacks to be proud and self-sufficient, arguing that they should develop their own institutions, pursue higher education, strive to attain property and wealth, and emulate the values of middle-class American whites. Furthermore, Pan-Africanists encouraged blacks to study and write about their own experiences and to teach racial pride to the younger generations.

The first edition of the *Crisis* was published in 1909, and soon became a leading periodical for African Americans. The journal sold for 10 cents a copy and grew to an average monthly circulation of eighty thousand, peaking at over ninety-five thousand in 1919.

Equally as important and influential as the NAACP was the National Urban League (NUL), the amalgamation of several black civil rights groups whose primary goal was to help African Americans who had recently migrated to northern cities find jobs. A nonpartisan, community-based organization, the NUL encouraged companies doing business in African American neighborhoods to help blacks enter the economic and social mainstream by hiring them as employees.

During World War I, many African Americans, like these members of the 369th Infantry regiment, enlisted in the military in the hopes that their service would earn them the respect of whites.

World at War

Even those who opposed accommodation were still prepared to exploit any opportunity to gain the respect of whites in order to finally gain their long-denied civil rights. One of these opportunities came in the unlikely form of a world war. In April 1917 the United States entered the war against Germany and the Austro-Hungarian Empire that had been raging in Europe since 1914. Many blacks were not eager to enter the military, seeing little to be gained from fighting a war so far from home. Still, DuBois and many other like-minded black leaders encouraged African Americans to enlist, believing that if blacks served their country, whites would honor that service and respect the rights African Americans had been denied for so long. Historian Cary D. Wintz writes, however, that from the start racist attitudes, segregation within the military, and hostilities between blacks and whites made service difficult for African Americans:

> Blacks hoped that the uniform they wore and the sacrifices they were willing to make for their country would win them some measure of respect and equal treatment. . . . From the beginning of the war, however, whites responded to black soldiers with hostility and fear. . . . They saw him [the black soldier] as a potentially dangerous element which in the future would have to be even more carefully kept under control.[6]

Despite such obstacles, many blacks served and distinguished themselves in combat during the war. Yet the expectations of DuBois and other black leaders were not borne out. Racist attitudes and racist violence did not vanish because of blacks' service to the country. In fact, during and following the war, blacks experienced a dramatic upsurge of violence directed at them.

Racial Violence

On July 2, 1917, for example, only three months after America's entry into the war, whites started a race riot in the community of East St. Louis that left thirty-nine blacks and nine whites dead. Throughout the South, lynchings continued unabated. Often black veterans were specifically targeted. The violent white-supremacy group known as the Ku Klux Klan, which had disbanded in 1880, reappeared in far greater numbers in 1915. In the years following World War I, the organization's membership grew to nearly 4 million.

White-incited race riots like the one in East St. Louis increased in number and severity. Underlying these violent attacks on black groups or black neighborhoods were a number of factors. Looming large was the fact that blacks, long excluded from labor unions, were being hired by companies, often as replacement workers when white employees went on strike. Furthermore, despite all the barriers, some blacks had managed to make economic gains and enter the middle class, earning them the jealousy of less well-off whites. And on occasion riots were stirred by some members of the press who espoused racist attitudes and openly called for violent action by whites against blacks.

The continuing violence angered many blacks who had spoken out in support of African Americans' participation in the war. In particular, the mistreatment of black veterans rankled leaders like DuBois. In an issue of the *Crisis* in 1919, DuBois pledged that, despite white America's unwillingness to acknowledge its debt to blacks, equality would be won:

> We return from the slavery of uniform which the world's madness demanded us to don to the freedom of civil garb. . . . This country of ours, despite all its better souls have done and dreamed, is yet a shameful land. . . . It *lynches*. . . . It *disenfranchises*. . . . It encourages *ignorance*. . . . It *steals* from us. . . . It *insults* us. . . . But it is *our* fatherland. . . . We will save [democracy in] the United States of America, or know the reasons why.[7]

Red Summer

Some African Americans decided that they had suffered long enough under the threat of violence at the hands of white racists. Many blacks, particularly veterans who had experienced combat in Europe, began to meet violence with violence.

The worst period of violence occurred in the summer of 1919. More than two dozen race riots broke out across the nation between April and October.

W.E.B. DuBois: The New Negro

Born on February 23, 1868, in Great Barrington, Massachusetts, William Edward Burghardt DuBois was educated in mixed-race schools during his youth. It was there he first experienced racist attitudes against him. A serious and good student, DuBois attended the prestigious Fisk University and then Harvard University, where he became the first black to receive a PhD from the school. He also traveled widely in Europe during his college years, doing post-graduate work in Germany in economics, history, and politics.

DuBois returned to New York in 1894 and began studying the conditions of blacks in New York. During this time, he came to believe that ignorance was at the root of racism and that scientific research would eventually prove that whites' fears of blacks were unfounded.

DuBois became a civil rights activist in his late twenties and early thirties. A renowned scholar by this time, he played important roles in the formation of African American civil rights organizations. In 1905 he helped found the Niagara Movement, which renounced Booker T. Washington's accommodationist policies and called for full civil liberties for blacks, an end to racial discrimination, and recognition of human unity. Then, in 1909 he helped found the National Association for the Advancement of Colored People (NAACP), an interracial organization focused on overturning the Jim Crow laws and pushing for racial integration.

Known as Red Summer because of the blood that ran in the streets during interracial clashes, the period saw hundreds of blacks and whites killed and many more injured. The worst incident occurred in Chicago. There, eighteen blacks and fifteen whites were killed, and five hundred people of both races were injured in the nearly two weeks of fighting.

A New Kind of Resistance

According to historian David Leverling Lewis, the race riots changed how people perceived the race problem in America:

They Came Marching Home

In February 1919 the African American Fifteenth Regiment of New York's National Guard returned to Harlem after fighting in World War I. The regiment's proud return for many was one of the harbingers of the New Negro movement, as described by David Leverling Lewis in his book *When Harlem Was in Vogue*.

On a clear, sharp February morning in 1919, on New York's Fifth Avenue, the men . . . marched home to Harlem. Their valor under fire . . . was legendary. . . . The staccato of leather on the Fifth Avenue macadam rose and fell to the deafening counterpoint of applause. . . . The tide of khaki and black turned west on 110th Street to Lenox Avenue, then north again into the heart of Harlem. . . . In front of the unofficial reviewing stand at 130th Street, [a] sixty-piece band broke into "Here Comes My Daddy" to the extravagant delight of the crowd. . . . "For the final mile or more of our parade," [one soldier recalled], "about every fourth soldier of the ranks had a girl upon his arm— and we marched through Harlem singing and laughing. . . ." The Hell Fighters were home.

The African American Fifteenth Regiment of New York's National Guard is welcomed home with a parade at the end of World War I.

"The 'race problem' became a definitively American dilemma in the summer of 1919, and no longer a remote complexity in the exotic South."[8] After Red Summer, in other words, race was clearly everyone's problem in America.

It was during and following the violence of the Red Summer that the term *New Negro* began to gain prominence in the black community. Although the term had come into being in an 1895 editorial to distinguish a new class of blacks who, unlike the former slaves, had gained some education and had attained a measure of prosperity, in 1919 the term took on a more militant connotation. Now, "New Negro" referred to a growing cadre of blacks who had rejected the accommodationist stance of Booker T. Washington in favor of a more radical black identity. Unapologetic, proud, and no longer willing to compromise on such issues as voting rights nor tolerate the abuse and prejudice of white racists, the New Negro was a force to be reckoned with. In an editorial in his newspaper the *Crusader*, African American activist Cyril V. Briggs wrote:

> The Old Negro [accommodationist] and his futile methods must go. After fifty years of him and his methods the Race still suffers from lynching, disenfranchisement, Jim Crowism, segregation and a hundred other ills. His abject crawling and pleading have availed the Cause nothing. . . . The New Negro now takes the helm.[9]

Choices for the New Negro

Various black organizations and leaders were eager to shape the identity of the New Negro as a means of determining the new direction for racial activism in the country. How the New Negro would confront racism and approach race relations in America became a grand debate among members of the African American community. However, as journalist George S. Schuyler wrote in the *Pittsburgh Courier*, the choices were limited:

> We must courageously face the fact that there are only three possible solutions to the so-called Negro problem. One is the wholesale emigration from these United States; another is segregation, either in ghettoes or a separate state; and third is amalgamation.[10]

In the 1910s and early 1920s, various African American leaders advocated one or another of these options and tried to gather widespread support for their solution to the race problem in America.

Segregation, of course, was already widely practiced throughout the country, especially in the South, where it had the force of law under the Jim Crow system. Separation, on the other hand, seemed to many a viable option, since it implied equality that was not to be found under Jim Crow.

Toward a Separate Nation

The notion of separatism gained popularity during the 1910s and 1920s, particularly among poor and working-class blacks. The most visible advocate of this strategy was Marcus Garvey. His organization, the Universal Negro Improvement Association (UNIA), established in 1914, promoted Pan-Africanism, economic and physical division between blacks and whites, and the establishment of a black nation located in Africa. As an example of economic separatism at work, UNIA established black-owned and -operated commercial enterprises in several states. These businesses included the Black Star Shipping Line and one of the first black-owned corporations, the Negro Factories Corporation. In addition, UNIA started a chain of restaurants, grocery stores, and laundries, a hotel, and a printing company.

Garvey's stated objective was, ultimately, to redeem the people of African descent from white oppression. As part of this vision, Garvey campaigned for blacks to leave America and return to Africa. This strategy, which was known as both the "Back to Africa" campaign and "Negro Zionism," was promoted through UNIA's newspaper, *Negro World*, a multilingual newspaper with international circulation. For a time, the movement enjoyed widespread support among African Americans, as indicated by UNIA's membership rolls. In 1919 UNIA had 2 million members; by 1921, there were over 4 million.

Near the peak of UNIA's popularity in 1920, the organization held its first international convention at Liberty Hall in New York from August 1 to 31. Attended by two thousand delegates from twenty-two countries, the convention elected Garvey the provisional president of Africa. The group also adopted a political platform titled the Declaration of Rights of the Negro People of the World, which declared the refusal of blacks all over the world to tolerate violence and inequality.

For a time, it seemed as though black separatism and nationalism would take hold in America. At UNIA's fourth annual international congress, for example, over 400,000 people in New York turned out in support. However, the separatist ideology ran counter to the philosophy of other leading black figures in the country, particularly the middle-class civil rights leaders such as DuBois.

Pushing for Assimilation

Those who opposed the black nationalists advocated assimilation and integration. DuBois and like-minded

Marcus Garvey, dressed as the self-proclaimed provisional president of Africa, rides to a UNIA rally in New York in 1922. His Back to Africa movement was short-lived.

leaders believed that separatism and nationalism—and particularly the idea of immigration to Africa—were impractical and counterproductive. They argued that the labor of black slaves had helped build America and that therefore America was their home just as much as it was whites'. What was lacking was social and political recognition and enforcement of blacks' rights, citizenship, and worth to the country. These leaders argued that an educated black elite—what DuBois called the Talented Tenth—would lead African Americans in their pursuit of civil rights. According to DuBois, this minority, having taken advantage of

Call to Arms

———————————■———————————

Marcus Garvey's period of influence in the United States was brief but powerful. He was able to organize millions of American blacks because he offered a defiant, uniting voice against white racism, as shown in this excerpt from an editorial printed in UNIA's *Negro World* on October 11, 1919, shortly after the race riots of Red Summer. The excerpt is reprinted in Theodore G. Vincent's collection *Voices of a Black Nation*.

> Once more the white man has outraged American civilization and dragged the fair name of the Republic before the court of civilized justice. . . .
>
> No mercy, no respect, no justice will be shown to the Negro until he forces other men to respect him. . . . Therefore, the best thing the Negro of all countries can do is prepare to match fire with hell fire. No African is going to allow the Caucasian to trample eternally upon his rights. We have allowed it for 500 years and now we have struck. . . .
>
> Let every Negro all over the world prepare for the new emancipation.

opportunities for education, should lead those who had not. According to historian Genna Rae McNeal,

> [DuBois] said that those who went to college had an obligation to give back to the community, to become leaders, and to be able to speak in circles where the masses were not going to be afforded an opportunity to participate. So the purpose of the Talented Tenth was not . . . snobbery but . . . service and responsibility.[11]

In reality, DuBois's term for this group was a misnomer because it implied that this privileged group constituted one-tenth of the black population. However, in 1917 only approximately two thousand out of 20 million blacks in America were attending college and few had achieved middle-class status or wealth and privilege. Thus, the Talented Tenth in truth represented only approximately one-tenth of 1 percent of the black population. Nevertheless, DuBois and like-minded intellectuals were adamant that educated middle-class blacks could and should use their relatively privileged status to lead the masses of African Americans toward integration and assimilation. DuBois believed that cultural development would spread from these elite blacks to others. "The Talented Tenth rises and pulls all that are worthy of saving up to their vantage ground,"[12] he wrote.

A Public Debate

As the best-known advocates for their respective movements, Garvey and DuBois came to be seen as being in opposition to each other. DuBois believed that black separatism could not work and that Garvey's philosophy was harmful to the goals and cause of assimilation. Meanwhile, Garvey felt that pinning one's hopes on the Talented Tenth was impractical and overlooked the needs of the poor and working class who made up the majority of the nation's black population.

The disagreement became highly personal. When Garvey met with leaders of the white-supremacist organization the Ku Klux Klan, who also argued for strict segregation, DuBois was alarmed and disgusted that a black leader would have anything to do with individuals who were responsible for terrorizing blacks. He called Garvey "without doubt the most dangerous enemy of the Negro race in America and the world. He is either a lunatic or a traitor."[13] Garvey, meanwhile, criticized DuBois for being out of touch with working-class and poor blacks: "Dr. Dubois . . . only appreciates one type of man, and that is the cultured, refined type which lingers around universities and attends pink tea affairs."[14]

In the end, DuBois prevailed—in part due to personal misfortune suffered by Garvey. Although UNIA was the largest mass movement of African Americans in the country's history, it relied heavily on Garvey's personal leadership and popularity. When Garvey was convicted in 1925 of mail fraud relating to sales of stock in the Black Star Shipping Line, he was sent to prison. After serving two years, Garvey was deported to his home country of

Garvey is led off to jail by U.S. marshals after his conviction for mail fraud in 1925. His conviction marked the end of his Negro Zionist political movement.

Jamaica. Without Garvey's leadership, UNIA lost influence among African Americans during the 1930s.

Unanswered Questions

Although Garvey and DuBois's debate over the future of the New Negro was the most public discussion, it was not the only one. Many other black intellectuals weighed in on how modern-day blacks should deal with the race issue. Thus, during the 1910s and 1920s, the New Negro movement was never a single, unified force for African Americans. However, as author Cary Wintz writes, the underlying elements of the strategies were similar:

> Some maintained that the essence of the New Negro was self-help, while others argued that the New Negro was ready to protest against discrimination or any abridgment of his civil rights. Still others insisted that the New Negro was Pan-African in outlook and determined to link the future of black Americans with the other colored peoples of the world. What all agreed on was the belief that large numbers of black Americans had become proud of their race, self reliant, and . . . that they were demanding their rights as American citizens.[15]

The questions of how to realize those rights remained part of the internal conflict of the New Negro movement throughout its existence. Furthermore, the questions and contradictions of how blacks should live and survive and what it meant to be black in America remained unresolved. Exploring these questions was essential to the work of many African American thinkers and artists of the 1920s and thus formed the creative background of the literary movement known as the Harlem Renaissance.

Chapter Two

Ushering in the Renaissance

The Harlem Renaissance was born out of opportunity. During the late 1910s and early 1920s, the leaders of the New Negro civil rights movement brought increasing public attention to the issues and problems relating to racial inequality in America.

At the same time, many younger white Americans looked to black America as a romantic and exotic culture untainted by cynicism and materialism. One consequence of this attitude was that black writers, composers, and artists found a new audience ready to listen to, absorb, and—they hoped—possibly act on the concerns of black Americans.

Literary Roots

This interest in African American culture was not unprecedented, although up to this time, whites had shown little interest in literature by African Americans. Book publishers—prior to the 1920s, at least—had reflected that lack of interest. There were few exceptions. The works of two notable African American writers, Paul Laurence Dunbar and Charles W. Chesnutt, had gained national attention in the 1890s; however, by the middle of the first decade of the twentieth century, Dunbar had died and in the generally hostile racial climate of the early twentieth century,

Chesnutt had largely been forgotten.

So it was that for African American writers, the literary land-scape during the early twentieth century was hostile and bleak. Between 1905, when Chesnutt's novel *The Colonel's Dream* had been published, and 1920, only five African Americans had succeeded in having major novels or collections of poetry published. Most of the black-authored work appeared not in book form but in newspapers and magazines such as the *Crisis* and *Opportunity*, as well as *Negro World*, the *Messenger*, the *Crusader*, and others. Demand among blacks for longer works was limited, mainly because books were too expensive for most working-class or poor African Americans to afford. Consequently, Cary Wintz writes,

> while the Renaissance would not emerge from a total literary vacuum, neither would it build on a well-established black literary tradition. The Harlem Renaissance would represent more accurately the birth of black literature than its rebirth.[16]

With so few works by black writers gaining the attention of white readers, it was music and the dramatic arts that played an important role in the beginning of the Harlem Renaissance.

Increasing Popularity

In the postwar years, plays, musicals, and revues featuring African American themes became increasingly popular with white audiences. These presentations were notably

Poet Paul Laurence Dunbar was one of only a handful of black American writers to gain literary fame before the Harlem Renaissance.

Blacks in Literature

———————————————————■———————————————————

In his 1924 book *The Gift of Black Folk*, W.E.B. DuBois examines the role of African Americans in literature, particularly American literature, including how portrayals of blacks changed over time.

> From the earliest times the presence of the black man in America has inspired American writers. . . .
>
> In the minds of these and other writers how has the Negro been portrayed? . . . In the days of Shakespeare and [Irish dramatist Thomas] Southerne the black man of fiction was a man, a brave, fine, if withal overtrustful and impulsive hero. Then with the slave trade he suddenly became a clown and dropped from sight. He emerged slowly beginning about 1830 as a dull stupid but contented slave. . . . Then, in the abolition controversy he became a victim, a man of sorrows . . . a crucified Uncle Tom. . . . Out of this today he is slowly but tentatively, almost apologetically rising—a somewhat deserving, often poignant, but hopeless figure; a man whose only proper end is dramatic suicide physically or morally. . . .
>
> And here we stand today. As a normal human being reacting humanly to human problems the Negro has never appeared in the fiction or the science of white writers, with a bare half dozen exceptions; while to the white southerner who "knows him best" he is always an idiot or a monster.

different from those seen in the past, however. Whereas blacks had been portrayed usually as comical or negative figures by white actors wearing makeup called blackface, now increasing numbers of African American actors, such as Paul Robeson, began portraying African Americans as serious individuals facing difficult problems with intelligence and dignity.

At the same time, less weighty entertainment, in the form of vaudeville performances by black musicians, became popular with white audiences. Presentations in traveling tent shows and in vaudeville houses in the big cities helped bring music such as ragtime, jazz, and blues, which had previously been mostly confined to the black community, into the mainstream.

Disillusionment

World events had worked to make younger white adults more inclined to look beyond their own traditions in seeking entertainment and culture. The overwhelming violence of World War I had left many young Americans disillusioned with the idea that European civilization and industrialization would lead to the betterment of humankind. Substantial numbers of Americans began to live nontraditional lifestyles and scorned conventional values. As David Leverling Lewis writes, these so-called bohemians, many of them writers or artists, were among those most powerfully drawn to African Americans precisely because blacks had long been excluded from the American mainstream:

> There existed a common belief that Western civilization had been badly wounded by runaway industrialism. . . . White rediscovery of Black Americans followed logically and naturally, for if the factory was dehumanizing, the university and the office stultifying, and the great corporation predatory, the Black American, excluded from the factory, university, office, and corporation, was the ideal symbol of innocence and revitalization.[17]

Particularly in the Manhattan neighborhood of Greenwich Village, considered the center of bohemian America, black culture became an object of fascination. Widely read white writers such as playwrights Eugene O'Neill and Sherwood Anderson began to portray African Americans in a serious light in their works, bringing blacks to the attention of an even wider audience. As Lewis notes, "The African American . . . indisputably moved to the center of Mainstream imagination with the end of the Great War."[18]

Opportunity for Change

This new interest in black culture among America's white writers soon caught the attention of several African American civil rights leaders, particularly those in the NAACP and NUL. These individuals, among them W.E.B. DuBois, Alain Locke, and Walter White, decided to capitalize on white interest in black culture to gain attention for African Americans' broader social and political concerns. They chose the arts as the avenue for advancement of their social agenda because most other means of progress were inaccessible. As Lewis writes,

> It was the brilliant insight of the men and women associated with the NAACP and NUL that, although the road to the ballot box, the union hall, the decent neighborhood, and the office was blocked, there were two untried paths that had not been barred . . . : arts and letters. They saw the small cracks in the wall of racism that could, they anticipated, be widened through the production of exemplary racial images in collaboration with white liberal philanthropy, the robust culture industry primarily located in New York, and artists from Bohemia.[19]

To some activists like DuBois, art was merely a tool for achieving civil rights goals. He believed that art should be serious, aesthetically pleasing, and most importantly educational. "Thus all Art is propaganda and ever must be,"[20] he wrote. Other black civil rights advocates such as Alain Locke and DuBois's assistant at the *Crisis*, author Jessie Redmon Fauset, differed from this approach. They believed that art was important and could achieve great things but that it should not be used as propaganda.

Nevertheless, these figures and many other like-minded black activists agreed that literature by African Americans, portraying African American life and culture in a positive light, would foster pride among young blacks. This would, they hoped, in turn further the agenda of the New Negro movement. According to this line of thought, positive portrayals, executed by members of the Talented Tenth, would show middle-class whites that African Americans shared their values and thus would eventually encourage whites to share in full the rights and benefits of American

An Exotic Stereotype

Through art and letters, New Negro leaders hoped to improve and reshape the racist, negative stereotypes of blacks. However, as Steven Watson writes in *The Harlem Renaissance*, Harlemania and the fascination with black culture created new stereotypes that were equally misguided.

> The fascination with Harlem was accompanied by the new objectification of the Negro as an exotic icon. . . . In line with 1920s fashion, the new stereotype incorporated many of the derogatory qualities previously attributed to Negroes, but they were now given a positive spin. The dangerously licentious, over-sexed figure of the earlier times was now idealized as being an uninhibited, expressive being. Racist images of the Negro as a barbaric jungle creature transformed into those of the noble savage, the natural man exuding animal vitality. . . . A symbol of the Jazz Age, the Negro was enlisted by high bohemia in its war against the [puritans, the middle-class,] and the Republicans who ruled the nation.

One of the most famous African American stereotypes created in the 1920s was the figure of Aunt Jemima.

Being promoted to icon status, however, did little to raise the financial fortunes of black Americans, nor did it break widespread Jim Crow laws.

society with their black compatriots. Locke wrote, "For the present, more immediate hope rests in the revaluation by white and black alike of the Negro in terms of his artistic endowments and cultural contributions, past and present."[21]

Alain Locke: Educator and Mentor

Among the best-known founders of the Harlem Renaissance was Alain Locke, a distinguished Harvard graduate who had been the first black Rhodes scholar, studying at Oxford University in England. He was employed as a professor at Howard University in Washington, D.C., the most respected black college in the country, where he provided classical education side by side with African and African American history. He also founded and edited *Stylus*, a literary magazine through which he nurtured and encouraged young black writers, including a then-unknown college student named Zora Neale Hurston, whose first short story Locke published.

In 1925 Locke was forced out of his job when he came out in support of the student movement protesting against conditions at the university. Following his dismissal, he moved to New York to help head up the arts movement. Locke wrote numerous essays on issues of race, becoming a rival in popularity to W.E.B. DuBois. He wrote extensively about the importance art would play in the advancement of race relations. He also acted as a mentor to many of the young Harlem Renaissance writers, including Langston Hughes and Countee Cullen.

Harvard graduate Alain Locke was among the best-known founders of the Harlem Renaissance. He mentored such Renaissance figures as Langston Hughes.

Lewis adds, however, that although the bohemians and New Negroes shared the view that art by and about African Americans could help bring about social change, the two groups differed in their ultimate goals:

New Negroes very much wanted full acceptance by Mainstream America. . . . For whites, art was a means to change society before they would accept it. For the blacks, art was the means to change society in order to be accepted into it.[22]

Nurturing the Renaissance

That art by refined and educated blacks could bring them into the fold of white culture—and encourage the masses of African Americans to better themselves and integrate as well—was an ideal shared by DuBois and many others associated with New Negro civil rights.

Beyond DuBois, the six individuals most vital to the development of the Harlem Renaissance were educator Alain Locke; writers Jessie Redmon Fauset, James Weldon Johnson, and Walter White; editor Charles S. Johnson; and financier Casper Holstein. With the exception of Holstein, all of these figures were middle-class, well-educated African Americans, paragons of DuBois's conception of the Talented Tenth. This small group set the stage for the Harlem Renaissance by creating an environment of support—financial and social—for new writers, and by creating opportunities for new black writers to be discovered and promoted to the public. Authors Claude McKay and Jean Toomer also helped usher in the Harlem Renaissance through the publication of books that for the first time in decades bridged the gap between black authors and white audiences.

Support Network

So closely was the Harlem Renaissance associated with the New Negro movement that in its early days it could be said to be headquartered in the offices of the NAACP and the NUL. After all, several of the people involved with the NAACP's and NUL's civil rights campaigns also worked with their affiliated magazines, the NAACP's *Crisis* and the NUL's *Opportunity: A Journal of Negro Life*. Through their affiliation with the NAACP and the *Crisis*, as well as through their outside connections and abilities, DuBois, *Crisis* literary editor Fauset, and authors Johnson and White helped create a support network for a new generation of writers.

Fauset was the unofficial mother figure for many of the new writers who became part of the Harlem Renaissance. A poet and writer who had aspired toward working in the publishing industry, Fauset ended up working as a teacher because publishing companies refused to hire her because of her race. Fauset applied the sense of literary merit she had developed as a teacher, which was helpful in identifying potential talent. As a critic and editor, Fauset proved invaluable in nurturing new writers.

Sometimes the contributions of a person went beyond literature. Such was the case with James Weldon Johnson, whose connections with white philanthropists brought in vital support for the NAACP's journal, the *Crisis*. This in turn allowed it to pay

Through his connections with philanthropists, James Weldon Johnson brought in vital financial support for the NAACP's journal, *Crisis*, which is still published today.

new writers for their contributions. Johnson's own literary contributions were important as well, although scholars point out that Johnson's first book, *The Autobiography of an Ex-Colored Man*, was published in 1912, well before the Harlem Renaissance got underway. The book is considered important for the example it provided to young Talented Tenth writers of how a black writer could overcome racial discrimination and adversity through hard work and talent.

In 1922 Johnson contributed even more directly to the Harlem Renaissance by compiling *The Book of American Negro Poetry*, which included works from older poets such as Paul Laurence Dunbar as well as contemporaries, including himself, DuBois, Fauset, and Claude McKay. Johnson's book gave momentum to the renaissance by proving to publishers that there was important black writing happening in the country. The book bolstered younger African American writers by demonstrating that publishers could eventually be made to see the market value of works by blacks.

Oftentimes, a writer's contribution went beyond his own work, taking the form of mentoring others and helping to get their work published. Walter White, like Johnson, was a well-known black writer. White became a New York celebrity after the publication in 1924 of his controversial first novel, *Fire in the Flint*. His fame gained him acquaintance with and access to some of the most illustrious figures in the arts, including prestigious publishers such as Alfred A. Knopf. The writer's wealthy, influential friends were helpful contacts for up-and-coming artists. In addition, White often gave much of his own time and money to help support new writers.

Opportunity

Many of these younger writers found the first outlet for their work in a journal called *Opportunity*, which was founded in 1923 by the National Urban League. *Opportunity*, just as the *Crisis* had, began publishing poetry, short stories, and essays. The two journals differed, however, in that the *Crisis* published works that tended to promote the New Negro movement's political agenda, whereas *Opportunity* focused on promoting African American culture, literature, and art. For this reason, many scholars agree that, from a literary standpoint, *Opportunity* was the most significant publication of the Harlem Renaissance.

Opportunity was founded and edited by Charles S. Johnson. Like DuBois, Johnson was pragmatic in his approach to literature in that he saw the growing interest in and romanticized notions of black culture among Greenwich Village bohemians as a chance for the advancement of African Americans. According to writer Arna Bontemps, "His subtle sort of scheming mind had arrived at the feeling that literature was the soft spot of the arts . . . and he set out to exploit it."[23]

Johnson maintained files on all African American writers in print and organized literary meetings and other events in Harlem at venues such as the 135th Street branch of the New York City Library. Johnson also understood that courting the publishing industry, which was largely controlled by whites, was vital to the success of any author. With this in mind, Johnson worked to bring black authors and leading whites from the publishing world together.

Johnson was arguably the most important supporter of the literary movement. He helped to find and arrange the support of new young black writers, nurtured writers, and organized literary events. According to Harlem Renaissance author Langston Hughes, Johnson did "more to encourage and develop Negro writers during the 1920's than anyone else in America."[24]

White Money and Negrotarians

The *Crisis* and *Opportunity* were crucial to the beginnings of the Harlem Renaissance. The magazines sought new writers, sponsored contests that featured monetary prizes, and arranged meetings between publishers, agents, and black writers. In doing so, these publications and the support network of the New Negro civil rights organizations changed the lives and careers of young writers and created a lively literary culture in Harlem.

The role played by Charles Johnson and Walter White, that of middleman between black artists and those who could support them financially, illustrates how important money was for the success of the Harlem Renaissance in general. Without funds, the civil rights organizations and their publications could not have supported the new movement. A few wealthy black benefactors, such as Casper Holstein, a successful entrepreneur whose profits in the gambling industry funded many of *Opportunity*'s awards and contests, were able to assist the movement. However, during the Harlem Renaissance the bulk of the money for supporting African American arts and letters came from whites. Nevertheless, it was Harlem Renaissance founders and supporters such as Alain Locke, James Weldon Johnson, and Walter White who performed a crucial role by convincing well-to-do whites to help support talented black writers and artists.

One Harlem Renaissance figure who understood the role of moneyed whites was Zora Neale Hurston, a young writer recruited to the movement through an *Opportunity* literary contest. At the same time, Hurston poked fun at those who provided the money and those who accepted it. Hurston coined the whimsical terms *Negrotarians* for whites who supported African American arts and *Niggerati* for the black literati and artists who benefited from their help.

Harlem Renaissance founder Walter White (center) served as a liaison between white patrons and black artists. He poses here with fellow NAACP activists Roy Wilkins (left) and Thurgood Marshall.

The support from whites came in a variety of forms besides the purely financial. According to Lewis, there were several categories of Negrotarians on whom the figures of the Harlem Renaissance relied. There were political Negrotarians, such as supportive journalists who reported on events and reviewed works; salon Negrotarians, who entertained and invited black artists to parties (although as exotic curiosities rather than talents); Lost Generation Negrotarians, who were utterly disillusioned by world leaders' failure to keep the peace and who saw African Americans as symbols of romance and rebellion against the status quo; and commercial Negrotarians such as editors and publishers who gambled on the commercial success of black literature to turn a profit.

The First Books

Still, historians stress that even though white donors in the early 1920s provided significant support for new writers in Harlem, the

Harlem Shadows by Claude McKay (left) and *Cane* by Jean Toomer (right) were among the first widely read books written by African Americans.

renaissance was at its heart an African American phenomenon. Two African American–authored books began a new trend in publishing. These were Claude McKay's collection of poetry titled *Harlem Shadows*, published in 1922, and Jean Toomer's *Cane*, a collection of fiction, sketches, and poetry, published in 1923.

What signaled the new trend was that these works were among the first widely read books of the twentieth century to have been written by African Americans. Until the appearance of these publications, most nationally published works about black people and the black experience in America had been written by whites. At the time, of the roughly sixty authors writing about blacks as subject matter in American fiction and poetry, fewer than eight (including Toomer and McKay) were black.

As was true of James Weldon Johnson, some scholars argue that McKay and Toomer should not be considered part of the Harlem Renaissance. This is because of their shared contempt for literature that served political ends and for literary politics, which were so much a part of the heritage of the Harlem Renaissance. Furthermore, McKay and Toomer both exiled themselves from the movement—McKay by leaving for Europe at the height of the renaissance and not returning until it was almost over and Toomer by refusing to identify himself as black.

Other critics argue that McKay and Toomer ushered in the Harlem Renaissance. These scholars point out that in their works McKay and Toomer set high standards for stylistic originality and displayed a commitment to the exploration of themes such as black identity. As Lewis writes, "[In their] dogged struggles simply to be themselves, they tested the outermost limits of what was possible for persons of African ancestry dedicated to the creative life."[25]

Toward a New Generation

What is beyond question is that having succeeded in gaining a national following themselves, McKay and Toomer helped pave the way for the younger poets and writers who are widely seen as central to the Harlem Renaissance. This new generation of writers—among the most prominent, Countee Cullen, Langston Hughes, Zora Neale Hurston, and Wallace Thurman—would form the backbone of the Harlem Renaissance literary movement.

Chapter Three

Voices of the Harlem Renaissance

The Harlem Renaissance began as a political movement whose leaders sought to harness the arts for the purpose of realizing their social and political goals. These African American leaders recruited young writers representative of the Talented Tenth, supporting them as they created works in which they explored black culture, heritage, and identity.

As these young writers developed, the bolder among them moved in directions the movement's founders had never envisioned, creating works that incorporated African American folklore and superstition, black slang and everyday language. Harlem ghetto life, including portrayals of poor and working-class blacks as well as criminals, prostitutes, and drug addicts, became a part of African American literature. The result was a body of work that was as vibrant as it was distinctive.

The New Generation

Though dozens of writers across the country became loosely associated with the Harlem Renaissance, those who defined it and became most closely identified with it were a small but gifted number. This group included Arna Bontemps, Countee Cullen, Langston Hughes, Zora Neale Hurston, Nella Larsen, and Wallace Thurman.

Recruited into the movement and given financial backing and editorial support by the likes of W.E.B. DuBois and Charles S. Johnson, these writers explored and wrote about African American experiences in a way no other writers before them had done. Presented with this opportunity, they created literary history.

There Is Confusion

Despite the significance of earlier works such as Claude McKay's *Harlem Shadows* and Jean Toomer's *Cane*, many scholars mark 1924 as the beginning of the Harlem Renaissance. In March of that year, *Opportunity* editor Charles S. Johnson arranged a literary gala event. The ceremonies were ostensibly to celebrate the publication of Jessie Fauset's first novel, *There Is Confusion*, which

Langston Hughes, here seen on the steps of his Harlem home in 1958, was one of the young rebels and self-styled "Niggerati" of the Renaissance.

the New Negro movement promoted as the first novel of the Harlem Renaissance. (Toomer's *Cane* had been a collection of stories rather than a novel, and McKay's work had been a collection of poetry.)

Fauset's book was the first novel portraying middle-class black life written by an African American. In 1922 Fauset had criticized white authors' attempts to write about black life. She had asked "whether or not white people will ever be able to write evenly on this racial situation in America."[26] In response to her own challenge, she wrote *There Is Confusion*, a portrayal of the life and relationships of a wealthy and ambitious black family.

Fauset had initially encountered resistance to her book from publishers, most of whom were white and accustomed to white authors writing about blacks. Most such books portrayed the sordid and exciting aspects of Harlem nightlife and featured black characters fulfilling popular stereotypes of blacks as exotic, rough, and lower class. Upon its publication by the respected firm of Boni and Liveright, *There Is Confusion* was touted by the leading figures of Harlem's literary community as a landmark in black literature. Moreover, Charles S. Johnson used its publication as an excuse to gather together the city's literary and publishing figures in order to announce the arrival of a new black literary movement.

Poet Countee Cullen began writing poetry at thirteen, earning him the nickname, the Wunderkind.

Zora Neale Hurston

Zora Neale Hurston came to Harlem from the South. She was born on January 7, 1891, in Eatonville, Florida, the first incorporated black community in America. Of Eatonville, where her father became mayor, Hurston said that African Americans lived away from the prejudices of white culture. Responding to Charles Johnson's call for black writers to come to Harlem, she came in 1925 with little more than a dollar in her pocket to be near the renaissance and to continue her education in anthro-

pology at Columbia, an education begun at Howard University and Barnard College. While Hurston worked on her fiction, she also studied the lives of African Americans in Harlem and, later, in the South.

Zora Neale Hurston mockingly referred to white art patrons as "Negrotarians" and black artists as "Niggerati."

The celebration of the publication of Fauset's novel was held at the Civic Club in Manhattan. Johnson's guest list included the cream of the black and white literary worlds. Prominent white downtown publishers, magazine editors, patrons, and writers—including such luminaries as Eugene O'Neill and H.L. Mencken—came together with the New Negro civil rights leaders and several fledgling black writers.

Despite being the ostensible reason for the celebration, Fauset and the publication of her book faded into the background of the evening's events. The real purpose of the evening was to announce the beginning of the Harlem Renaissance.

Alain Locke spoke at length about the promise of the new generation of black writers and served as master of ceremonies, introducing speakers such as Charles S. Johnson, James Weldon Johnson, and W.E.B. DuBois, who echoed the theme. In his speech, DuBois also promised the young writers in the audience that, although his generation had been denied its authentic voice, theirs would not.

The dinner was a pageant and a successful business event. For the first time, the whites and blacks involved in the literary world were able to socialize and make potential business connections. Out of the meeting of these literati came an offer from *Harper's* magazine to publish work by Countee Cullen, the formation of a Writer's Guild, and an offer to Charles Johnson by the popular white magazine the *Survey Graphic* to devote an entire issue to works about African American life.

The Survey Graphic

The *Survey Graphic's* unprecedented offer was exciting. At Johnson's request, Locke edited the issue, working with Johnson to solicit contributors. In their search for writers and material, Locke and Johnson wanted to make sure that the work included in the collection fit the artistic and political agenda of the New Negro movement. The writing had to be polished and refined, reflecting middle-class values and avoiding racial stereotypes or what they considered vulgar or low depictions of blacks and their culture. The goal was to convey the idea that middle-class blacks were no different than their white counterparts.

The *Survey Graphic's* African American issue was published in March 1925 and sold out two printings. This made it the magazine's most popular issue ever. The issue was added to, revised, and reprinted several months later as a book titled *The New Negro*. Locke's dedication in that volume, "To the Younger Generation," expressed his hope that the book would help inspire up-and-coming black writers and artists. Locke's foreword to *The New Negro* pointed to the literary movement, "the Negro Renaissance," as it was initially termed, as representative of a new revolutionary state of mind and course of action in the country:

Visual Artists of
the Harlem Renaissance

███

Although the Harlem Renaissance was primarily a literary phenomenon, the other arts went through a similar period of experimentation and growth at the time. As this excerpt from the Studio Museum in Harlem's book *Harlem Renaissance Art of Black America* describes, as black writers of the literary movement had, African American visual artists, including painters and sculptors, turned to African themes in their work.

> [Harlem Renaissance leaders] directed young black artists to African art as an important source of aesthetics and iconography that would be meaningful for their race. . . . Among those who responded . . . were four Black artists. . . .

> Aaron Douglas . . . chose to observe aspects of African rituals expressed in dance and everyday life and incorporated the iconography into his own work. . . . Meta Warrick . . . inventively interpreted African folktales in her sculptures, bringing new insights to the portrayal of neo-African themes in American art. Palmer Hayden became the principal artist to communicate Black folklore from the South through his paintings and to express visually the native customs of Southern blacks. . . . William H. Johnson . . . established himself as a special interpreter of the culture of Black people in the South and of the primitive peoples of several European countries. . . .

> The wisdom, insightful artistry, and creative will of these four artists helped establish a new tradition among Black American artists that affirmed both their individual and racial identities. . . . During the flowering years of the Renaissance the work of these four individuals helped to direct the artistic genius of a people whose place was Harlem.

As in India, in China, in Egypt, Ireland, Russia, Bohemia, Palestine and Mexico, we are witnessing the resurgence of a people. . . . Negro life is not only establishing new contracts and founding new centers, it is finding a new soul. . . . We have, as the heralding sign, an unusual outburst of creative expression. There is a renewed race-spirit that consciously and proudly sets itself apart. Justifiably then, we speak of the offerings of this book embodying those ripening forces as culled from the fruits of the Negro Renaissance.[27]

The publication of *The New Negro* was of major significance to the black literary community. This was particulary so for the writers whose work appeared in the book, since for many of them it was the first time they were being published nationwide.

In soliciting the material from black writers, Locke and Johnson encouraged writers, no matter where they were living, to move to Harlem to take part in the renaissance. To make it possible for them to afford the expense of uprooting their lives and coming to the city, Johnson arranged for the new arrivals to be looked after by his secretary and her network of friends. These dedicated individuals provided loans, food, and places to stay until the new arrivals were able to find jobs or obtain grants or awards that would cover their living expenses.

Opportunity Awards

Fortunately for the most talented among these young authors, such awards were available. Soon after the Civic Club dinner, *Opportunity* established annual literary awards to honor promising new writers. The *Crisis* followed suit shortly afterward.

The *Crisis* and *Opportunity* awards in 1924 and 1925 were highlights of the black literary scene and significant landmarks to the Harlem Renaissance. At the award ceremonies were honored the brightest stars of the new generation whose works had been published in the journals' pages. Honorees included Countee Cullen, Langston Hughes, and Zora Neale Hurston.

In Search of Black Identity

From the beginning of their careers, these and other young African American writers explored interrelated themes that for a

Much of Langston Hughes's work explores the theme of dual identity among African Americans. Hughes encouraged American blacks to embrace their African heritage.

time helped define and unify the Harlem Renaissance. Among the most prevalent and important of these themes was the complex nature of black identity in America. One element of this theme that had long consumed African American authors was the duality of black identity. For example, as early as 1903 W.E.B. DuBois had noted in *The Souls of Black Folk* that African Americans were often confused and troubled by the inherent conflict of being both black and American:

> One ever feels his two-ness—an American, a Negro; two souls, one dark body, whose dogged strength alone keeps it from being torn asunder. The history of the American Negro is the history of this strife—this longing to attain

Countee Cullen, the Wunderkind

■

Countee Cullen, whose birthplace is unknown because he gave many different answers over the years, was born on March 30, 1903. Abandoned by his mother and never knowing his father, he was raised by his grandmother until her death when he was fifteen. He was then taken in by a Harlem minister named Frederick Cullen and his wife. Although the couple never adopted him, he took their family name.

Cullen began writing formal poetry while attending a mostly white high school. He published his first poem at sixteen years old and one of his still best known, "Life's Rendezvous," in his high school literary journal when he was eighteen.

While studying at New York University and winning a stream of awards at the college, he began attending literary events in Harlem. There he met several African American figures, including Jessie Fauset and *Opportunity* editor Charles Johnson's secretary. With their encouragement, he began reciting his poetry to the audiences. And soon both the *Crisis* and *Opportunity* began publishing his poetry. Thereafter, national magazines such as *Harper's Quarterly* and *American Mercury* carried his work. By age twenty-two, when his first collection, *Color*, was published, he had become among the most famous black writers in America.

self-conscious manhood, to merge his double self into a better and truer self.[28]

One way black authors dealt with this dual identity was by recognizing, exploring, and celebrating their African heritage. Mainstream white political thinkers in America portrayed Africa as being a continent in decline. However, according to Harlem Renaissance scholar Nathan Irvin Huggins, black writers looked to Africa as a place of strength, dignity, and importance that had been abused by centuries of Western colonialism. Huggins writes,

Afro-Americans had to search beyond their American experience for the roots of self and culture. Africa necessarily became crucial to their sense of self. For a black American to answer the question of identity, he had to resolve for himself what Africa was and what Africa meant to him.[29]

One of the first among the new black writers to take up this theme was poet Langston Hughes. As early as his senior year in high school, in a poem titled "The Negro Speaks of Rivers," Hughes expressed pride in his African heritage and its roots in ancient civilizations that grew up along rivers such as the Euphrates (in modern-day Iraq) and the Nile (which runs through Egypt).

Against Racism

Pride in their racial identity also led many writers to give voice to the anger, sorrow, and frustration that blacks felt over the racism they routinely experienced in America. Anger over racism was, of course, not new. One of the first published works along these lines had been Claude McKay's "If We Must Die," which was a solemn battle cry against the race riots of the Red Summer of 1919. However, the works of younger poets and writers, such as Countee Cullen's "Incident," addressed more personal assaults of racism. In the poem, Cullen recalls his experience of visiting Baltimore when he was eight years old. While riding a streetcar, a young boy called him "Nigger." The brief incident marred the entire trip for him. In the final stanza Cullen notes that whatever other experiences he had over the course of seven or eight months, he remembers only that one.

Exploring Taboo Themes

As the new generation of African American writers gained experience and began publishing their works, several of them, including Langston Hughes, Zora Neale Hurston, Arthur Fauset, Wallace Thurman, and others, began pushing the boundaries of taste as defined by DuBois and the Talented Tenth. They did this by writing about life outside the relatively privileged world of the educated black elite. By portraying the lives, the language, the music, and the experiences of the majority of the people around them—the Harlem poor and working class—the writers offended

Wallace Thurman and others like him wrote about the lives of Harlem's poor and working-class blacks.

and upset their supporters, who largely believed that such writing hindered the efforts of the New Negro movement to garner respect from whites.

With young Wallace Thurman—known as the wild child of the Harlem Renaissance—as their unofficial leader, this group of writers and artists became associated with a house at 267 136th Street in Harlem that Thurman and Hurston mockingly named Niggerati Manor. Niggerati Manor became the headquarters for those who were in revolt against the elitist Talented Tenth dictates of DuBois, Locke, and the others who had nurtured the Harlem Renaissance during its infancy. Although these writers had benefited from the New Negro movement's support network, they shared the belief that the Talented Tenth's leaders were short-sighted and condescending toward the majority of blacks. Arthur Fauset said that the privileged old guard looked down on people "who didn't dress properly, whose finger nails were dirty, and who didn't eat properly, and whose English was not good."[30]

Fauset, in fact, was correct. DuBois, Locke, and other likeminded intellectuals made no secret of their distaste for stories about ghetto life or ghetto people. They objected to what they considered the vulgar slang and coarse language used routinely by the poor and the working class. They did not like lowly entertainment such as jazz or the blues, preferring instead classical music by European composers or the spirituals sung in black churches. The denizens of Niggerati Manor, however, said that they found in down-to-earth black culture beauty and a wealth of inspiration for their art.

Fire!!

As a demonstration of their emerging independence, in 1926 Thurman edited a collection of avant-garde writing titled *Fire!!* which was intended as a shocking alternative to the depictions of the black middle-class encouraged by the Talented Tenth. Watson describes the subject matter as celebrating "jazz, paganism, blues, androgyny, unassimilated black beauty, free-form verse, homosexuality—precisely the 'uncivilized' features of Harlem [working-class] culture that the Talented Tenth preferred to ignore."[31]

Fire!! contained the boldest and most experimental work by many prominent Harlem writers and artists, including the Niggerati Manor contingent—Hughes, Hurston, and Thurman—as well as visual artists Aaron Douglas and Richard Bruce Nugent. Hughes said that the material in *Fire!!* represented Harlem Renaissance figures who were interested in "those elements within the race which are still too potent for easy assimilation . . . [and which the elites want] hidden until they no longer exist."[32]

As its editor had intended, *Fire!!* horrified many of the Talented Tenth, who believed it was evidence of the decline of the Harlem Renaissance. Consequently, many of those who had contributed works to the anthology were snubbed by other blacks. In particular, middle-class blacks and critics, the very people who might have purchased

Aaron Douglas supplied many of the illustrations for the 1926 anthology, *Fire!!*, a collection of writings that celebrated the seamier side of Harlem life.

the book or promoted it, ignored it. Although *Fire!!* had been conceived as the first installment of a literary journal, it died after one issue.

Color Discrimination

Despite the lack of success of *Fire!!* the writers who had contributed to it continued to explore taboo subject matter and themes in their work. Langston Hughes, for example, incorporated the rhythm and themes of the blues into his poetry. Zora Neale Hurston wrote about superstitions and folklore, using the idiom of the people she wrote about. The young rebels saw beauty and truth in such honest portrayals of black life, and they strove to portray African Americans in ways that ignored what they considered the airs being put on by the Talented Tenth.

Wallace Thurman and others explored an explosive issue, that of color discrimination among blacks themselves. Among urban African Americans, those with lighter skin were generally treated better and seen as more acceptable and more attractive than those with darker skin. An elaborate vocabulary arose to describe the various skin tones, and there was even discrimination based on these variations.

Color discrimination was a prevalent and welcome theme among the Talented Tenth elites, as long as it dealt with whites discriminating against blacks. "Passing" was an issue of importance to most African Americans, however, as those whose skin was light enough to pass as white could benefit from the advantages of full citizenship, whereas most others were subject to discrimination and/or segregation. Several novels by Harlem Renaissance writers discussed this phenomenon, including Nella Larsen's popular 1929 novel *Passing.* The protagonist in *Passing* is a light-skinned black woman whose racial identity is unknown even to her husband.

Nevertheless, many blacks were upset when authors discussed how light-skinned blacks looked down on those with darker skin. In 1929 Thurman's novel *The Blacker the Berry* was published. *The Blacker the Berry* dealt with prejudice and discrimination based on skin tone within the black community. Because many African Americans considered this phenomenon a shameful secret within their community, they were angered by any book that exposed it.

Portraying Reality

Negative criticism of works by the more adventurous Harlem Renaissance figures was common. Moreover, the discomfort of DuBois, Locke, and others of the Talented Tenth went beyond concern for how such writing affected their political agenda. Lewis writes that these African American leaders saw the writing that came out of Niggerati Manor as a personal affront: "Condemnation [of such work] by the Talented Tenth and others stemmed from racial sensitivity from sheer mortification at seeing uneducated, crude, and scrappy black men and women depicted without tinsel and hope."[33]

Some Talented Tenth figures also complained that works about lower-class blacks played into the hands of racist white publishers who were reluctant to publish books that portrayed blacks in a positive light. Such works, they said, tended to confirm in these publishers' minds the view of black life as sordid and low. DuBois argued that the publishers fed into racism by "refusing to handle novels that portray Negroes of education and accomplishment, on the grounds that these characters are no different from white folk and therefore not interesting."[34]

In defense of such unapologetically authentic portrayals of black life, in 1926 Langston Hughes wrote an essay titled "The Negro Artist and the Racial Mountain," which was published in the *Nation*. He wrote, "We younger Negro artists who create now intend to express our individual dark-skinned selves without fear or shame."[35]

Two prime examples of this unapologetic writing were Hughes's own 1927 collection of poetry titled *Fine Clothes to the Jew* and Claude McKay's novel *Home to Harlem*, published in 1928. *Fine Clothes to the Jew* contains poetry about the lives of poor and working-class blacks expressed in the idiom of everyday speech. Hughes also wrote about black folk music and incorporated the themes and feel of blues music (considered "low" culture by the Talented Tenth) into his writing. He also portrayed scenes of sex, physical abuse, alcoholism, and other lurid elements he saw around him in the streets of Harlem.

McKay's novel *Home to Harlem* was published in America, although the author had been living in France since 1922 when he had left to escape what he saw as the country's pervasive racism. Although McKay had been away from Harlem for years,

Langston Hughes, Poet

———————◼———————

Langston Hughes was born in Joplin, Missouri, on February 1, 1902. Raised by his grandmother, a central and influential figure in his life, he had an unsettled upbringing, moving around a great deal and meeting many different kinds of people.

He began writing poetry at age thirteen. In his senior year of high school he wrote "When Sue Wears Red," about a black junior high school girl at a dance wearing a red dress. It was the first of his many poems to deal with race.

After he graduated high school in 1919, Hughes traveled by train to Mexico to spend the year with his father, who lived there. During the trip he wrote "The Negro Speaks of Rivers," a poem expressing pride in the ancient nobility of African American heritage, which he dedicated to W.E.B. DuBois. Hughes sent this poem to Jessie Fauset at the *Crisis* a few months after writing it. Fauset showed it to DuBois and they decided to publish it. When Hughes arrived in New York the following year in 1921 to study mining at Columbia University, Fauset invited him to come to the NAACP offices and meet with her and DuBois.

Drawn into the early days of the Harlem Renaissance literary movement, Hughes quit college after a year to write, making his living as a servant on an international freighter based on the Hudson River. On his first freighter trip abroad, he went to Africa, where he visited the Azores, Nigeria, and the Belgian Congo, seeing the effects of European colonialism on native Africans. Deeply affected by what he had seen, he returned in October 1924 to find himself among the first recipients of awards given by the *Crisis* and *Opportunity.*

he recalled it well and in *Home to Harlem* brazenly explored the neighborhood's underworld, including its street life, jazz venues, and back rooms, where drinking, drugs, gambling, and prostitution were common.

The novel received praise from many reviewers, both black and white, and also proved that there was a large audience for honest and unflinching depictions of African American life: *Home to Harlem* became the first black-authored book to become a national best seller. Not surprisingly however, the book was reviled by many Talented Tenth blacks and even others like Marcus Garvey, who in *Negro World* accused McKay and the other rebel writers of "prostituting their intelligence, under the direction of the white man, to bring out and show up the worst traits of our people."[36] DuBois and Garvey were in rare agreement on such writing. For his part, DuBois said that reading the sordid details of Harlem street life in McKay's book made him feel "distinctly like taking a bath."[37]

Nigger Heaven

However, the book that received the most negative attention from Talented Tenth critics, *Nigger Heaven*, was not even authored by a black writer but by white author Carl Van Vechten. Van Vechten was a Greenwich Village bohemian who had become one of the most influential Negrotarians. Prominent in social circles inhabited by publishers and literati, he helped black writers such as Langston Hughes get published. Van Vechten also had many friends among black writers and artists. In fact, he spent so much time in Harlem that he was like an unofficial tour guide, able to show white people the real black Harlem. Because of his intimacy with the neighborhood and the people in it, his book was considered by many critics to be the first widely published insider's look at Harlem, despite having been written by a white person.

Set in Harlem in the early 1920s, *Nigger Heaven* was in many ways a conventional melodrama, but it portrayed the suffering and aspirations of poor and working-class blacks with honesty and empathy. However, *Nigger Heaven* was very unpopular with DuBois, Locke, Cullen, and a large number of black readers because of its portrayal of aspects of black culture that they believed reinforced negative black stereotypes and therefore damaged the prospects for integration that members of the New Negro movement had sought for so long.

Despite its many black critics, the book became an instant best seller. The book was responsible for introducing African American life and Harlem to a wider audience than any black-authored

Nigger Heaven

■

Although decried by many critics, Carl Van Vechten's *Nigger Heaven* was one of the most popular books of the 1920s, going through nine printings in a few months. It helped to popularize Harlem and the Harlem Renaissance writers. Excerpted below is a passage from the book printed in Steven Watson's *The Harlem Renaissance*.

Nigger Heaven! Byron moaned. Nigger Heaven! That's what Harlem is. We sit in our places in the gallery of this New York theatre and watch the white world sitting down below in the good seats in the orchestra. Occasionally they turn their faces up towards us, their hard, cruel faces, to laugh or sneer, but they never beckon. It never seems to occur to them that Nigger Heaven is crowded, that there isn't a seat, that something has to be done. It doesn't seem to occur to them

either, he went on fiercely, that we sit above them, that we can swoop down from this Nigger Heaven and take their seats. No, they have no fear of that! Harlem! The Mecca of the New Negro! My God!

Author Carl Van Vechten helped to introduce white readers to the writers of the Harlem Renaissance.

publication had. In addition, *Nigger Heaven* was in large part responsible for greatly increasing whites' curiosity and interest in Harlem during the mid-1920s. The book led many whites to go to Harlem for the first time and helped stoke the fervor of what would be called Harlemania. As author Cary Wintz writes,

> [*Nigger Heaven*] was the most important single event in creating the Negro craze. . . . More than any other single individual, [Van Vechten] created the Negro vogue. Following the publication of the book, white middle-class America eagerly devoured anything with black flavor to it.[38]

Breaking Away

By the late 1920s, almost no book coming out of Harlem escaped criticism by either the Talented Tenth or the rebellious avant-garde. This growing rupture between the more daring black writers of the renaissance and the Talented Tenth leadership marked an important turn in the direction of the Harlem Renaissance. While some like Charles S. Johnson supported this breaking away, others, particularly DuBois, resisted.

Novels by DuBois, James Weldon Johnson, Walter White, and a volume of Countee Cullen's poetry appeared to continue the tradition of Talented Tenth writing, but none fared particularly well critically. Meanwhile, the breakaway writers grew in reputation and power. Although *Fire!!* printed only one issue, another avant-garde magazine, *Harlem*, took its place in 1928. Only two issues of *Harlem* appeared, but to the chagrin of DuBois and others, the magazine even received the support of two Talented Tenth members, Alain Locke and Walter White.

Whatever the feelings of those who had brought the Harlem Renaissance into being, by the late 1920s and early 1930s, the literary movement was primarily in the hands of the young rebels rather than of the founders. In these years, some of the most significant work by Harlem Renaissance authors came into print and changed black literature. At the same time, Harlem was becoming the focus of white attention in ways the founders of the renaissance had not anticipated.

Chapter Four

Harlemania

Harlem achieved notoriety in the early 1920s as its population of African Americans grew and the social and literary movements centered there gained momentum. However, in the mid-to-late 1920s the allure of Harlem grew tremendously. Not only were black artists and entertainers drawn there, but whites—bohemians, the trend conscious, and the merely curious—thronged to Harlem as it gained cachet as the place to be. A fad—known to historians as "Harlemania"—developed. According to Cary D.Wintz,

> The glamour and excitement that made Harlem a Mecca for black writers also attracted the attention of white New Yorkers who began regular pilgrimages to the ghetto in search of its exotic nightlife.[39]

During its peak of popularity in the mid-1920s to early 1930s, Harlem was like two separate worlds in one. The world of the poor and working-class blacks who made up the majority of the community's residents was far different than that of the Talented Tenth elite who lived there and the white revelers and bohemians who came north in the evenings to experience the exotic culture of the neighborhood. However, the arts and entertainment scene in Harlem was so pervasive and so important to every aspect of life during this period that it touched everyone, rich or poor, black or white.

The Renaissance and Harlemania

Among the artists and leaders of the Harlem Renaissance, the fad known as Harlemania met with widely different responses. Despite the popularity and celebration that Harlemania brought to black entertainers, many of the New Negro movement's leaders such as W.E.B. DuBois and the rest of the Talented Tenth frowned upon it, preferring the "high" culture of opera, classical music, and the sober events of high society to what they saw as the decadence of the fad: its music, and its associations with sex, drugs, and alcohol. Conversely, most of the notable Harlem Renaissance writers, including Langston Hughes, Wallace Thurman, and Zora Neale

African Americans in a Harlem nightclub watch as a couple performs one of the latest dance crazes. Whites were also regular patrons of Harlem's hot spots.

Jive Talk and the Zoot Suit

The jazz culture of the Harlem Renaissance deeply penetrated American culture. As Bruce M. Tyler writes in his book *From Harlem to Hollywood,* one of the most notable effects in popular culture was the jazz-influenced language and fashion of the 1930s and 1940s:

> Black jive developed out of the jazz and nightlife culture. The Harlem Renaissance cultural and intellectual leaders in the nightlife and jazz world in the 1920s produced a highly sophisticated subculture with its own language and dress codes that filtered increasingly into the general population of whites and blacks. Black society usually was the first to accept the trends, and "hep" whites, usually those in the entertainment world, soon followed, bringing along white party-goers who also participated in the jive and jazz culture. . . .
>
> Black slang or jive talk became popular in the late 1930s and early 1940s. [Jazz musician] Cab Calloway led the way with his "Harlemese" language or jive talk. . . . [On a radio program] Calloway and several band members answered questions about music and musicians. They "shucked and jived" by speaking the "slick" and highly developed Harlemese subculture street and entertainment language. Actually a

Hurston, indulged fully in and wrote about the Harlem nightlife, making its appeal even greater. Wintz writes,

> Harlem writers avidly embraced the music and nightlife of Harlem's cabarets . . . [and] Harlem's black bohemia formed the essential backdrop to the black literary Renaissance. Young black writers submerged themselves in the primitive black culture that flourished in the ghetto's speakeasies, gin houses, and jazzrooms. There all of Harlem converged: the prostitute, the washwoman, the petty gangster, the poet, and the intellectual shared the blues and swayed to the beat of the jazz musicians.[40]

dialect in its own right, it became the language of the jazz world. . . . Many black and white entertainers took a great deal of pride in their jive as the language of their profession.

The Zoot suit became the preeminent code of dress for the extreme hipster during World War II . . . Zoot suits, jitter-bug pants [suits without the jacket], and New York–style shoes became popular in the black urban centers during the war. Jive, jazz, jitterbugging, Zoot suits, jitterbuggers, and Zoot suiters became a symbol for the city slicker.

Flamboyant black bandleader Cab Calloway sports a white Zoot suit at a 1935 Harlem gig.

Still, Harlemania and the nightlife were in many ways discon-nected from the everyday lives of most of the residents of the city. Most Harlem residents did not participate in the late nights and parties; few could afford to do so, and were not interested in such activities in any case. As David Leverling Lewis writes:

People rose in Harlem each day to go to work, many of them before the last white revelers had careened home-ward. The great majority never saw the interior of a night-club. Many would have spurned a free night on the town from religious or moral certainty that the devil himself was the club proprietor. Like any young immigrant community, most of Harlem was sober and hardworking. Those with the money and inclination to roam [the streets] until the crack of dawn probably represented well under 10 percent of the total.[41]

The Soundtrack to the Renaissance

Common to the two worlds of Harlem was African American art, theater, and, particularly, music. During the late nineteenth and early twentieth centuries as southern blacks came north, they brought with them the spirituals and work songs they had sung since slave times and rhythms that originated in Africa. These elements, along with ragtime, jazz, and blues, combined in the 1920s to become the core of Harlem's culture and community life. Music scholar Samuel A. Floyd Jr. writes,

> Music was flourishing everywhere. . . . Cabarets did a booming business with prohibition liquor and popular music; concert life was active and stimulating. The common black folk were frequenting the cabarets, and so too were the intellectuals after attending concerts of the New York Philharmonic Orchestra and the Metropolitan Opera. But Harlem was in the center of the movement.
>
> The white show world of downtown New York, where a few black musicians performed and where black shows were also presented, was active, but after hours everyone, white and black, went to Harlem to hear black music.[42]

With its burgeoning nightclubs, speakeasies, and dance halls, its jazz and blues, and its atmosphere of celebration and liberation in the 1920s, Harlem became a fashionable destination among the white bohemian thrill seekers and the young middle-class adults eager to shock what they considered the sober, staid establishment.

The impact of Harlem's wild popularity was felt throughout Manhattan and became renowned through much of America and even across the Atlantic in Europe—particularly in Paris—where many Harlem dancers and jazz musicians were welcomed and celebrated. During these years, it seemed everyone knew about Harlem.

The Club Life

For many who lived in the neighborhood and thousands who traveled uptown each week, Harlem provided a seemingly limitless array of entertainments and distractions. For a time, the whites who were interested in Harlem's culture had mainly been the patrons of artists and writers—what Zora Neale Hurston somewhat mockingly called the Negrotarians. However, in the mid- to late 1920s, Harlem at night became a favorite spot for adventurous whites to find entertainment. From downtown they would drive or take the "A" train uptown to spend the late hours of the evening and early hours of the morning going to nightclubs, seeing shows, listening to jazz or blues, and dancing and drinking bootleg liquor. Among white New Yorkers, Harlem was celebrated as a wild spot. Popular white stand-up comedian and Harlem regular Jimmy Durante noted:

Revelers ring in the new year of 1938 at Harlem's Cotton Club while Cab Calloway sets the beat. The Cotton Club was the best-known Harlem nightclub.

You go sort of primitive up there with the bands moaning blues like nobody's business, slim, bare-thighed brown-skin gals tossing their torsos, and the Negro melody artists beating down something terrible on the minor notes.[43]

Many of those who went to Harlem also did so because of the availability of illegal liquor. The Volstead Act, which in 1919 had outlawed the sale or manufacture of alcoholic beverages, created a clandestine industry run by organized crime. Moreover, white authorities tended to ignore the sale of alcohol in black neighborhoods like Harlem, as long as such illegal activities did not migrate to white districts.

Though the availability of liquor drew whites to Harlem, even here, racial barriers still existed and were enforced. This was particularly true at the clubs that charged the highest admission fees and which were often owned by whites. Mixing between blacks and whites, however, was more common in some of the less expensive gin mills, speakeasies, and dance halls that were black owned and at a few run by whites who did not care about the race of their customers.

The high-end clubs catered to white patrons who wanted adventure but not integration. The entertainment often featured jazz orchestras and elaborate floor shows, most of it provided by African Americans who would not have been allowed to enter through the front doors. In these clubs, distinctions between skin tone determined who among African Americans did which job. Lighter-skinned black female dancers provided the entertainment while darker-skinned blacks waited tables and served as busboys.

The Cotton Club was the best known and gaudiest of the Harlem nightclubs. It featured elegantly dressed tables, banquets filled with American and foreign cuisine, comedians, and elaborate shows (written by whites) featuring the orchestras of Cab Calloway and Duke Ellington. Of all the clubs, the Cotton Club was particularly segregated and was considered a white sanctuary, popular among white Harlem newcomers who wanted to "experience" Harlem without having to mix with those who lived and worked there. As Watson writes, "The Cotton Club allowed the timid and the well-heeled to cautiously dip their stylishly shod feet into the roiling waters of primitive uptown."[44]

Speakeasies and Rent Parties

Not all visitors to Harlem were so timid. Many of the residents of Harlem and the more adventurous visitors found entertainment in the speakeasies—essentially illegal bars—which although less chic than the exclusive nightclubs were more affordable. These establishments were frequently unmarked, located down the side streets and often in cellars. They attracted working-class blacks who were inclined to partake of Harlem's nightlife as well as the black musicians and entertainers who had finished their performances at the white-owned clubs but were not allowed to patronize the very places in which they entertained.

On busy nights, the speakeasies were densely crowded. Customers drank cheap bootleg liquor and often indulged in readily available drugs such as marijuana and cocaine. On the wooden floors revelers danced to ragtime and the blues, packed so tightly that often people had to dance in one place—called "dancing on a dime." The celebrations got started late, and frequently got more raucous at two or three in the morning. The revelry often lasted until seven in the morning.

In addition to frequenting the speakeasies, many people also attended Harlem's rent parties. Such parties were homegrown working-class forms of entertainment that were readily available on most late nights in Harlem. Ever since blacks had first moved into Harlem, they had paid inflated rents; by the 1920s, the typical black-inhabited apartment often cost its residents nearly half of their monthly income. If renters could not pay the landlord on time, they were threatened with eviction.

To keep themselves from being put out on the street, people would throw so-called rent parties in their apartment. The living spaces would be cleared out, chairs borrowed, and cheap food prepared. Simple printed announcements were passed out, and those who showed up paid admission of 10 to 50 cents to drink, eat, socialize, and dance all night to music on the radio or perhaps to live music played by a blues musician hired for the occasion. Langston Hughes recalled the atmosphere of those parties:

Almost every Saturday night when I was in Harlem I went to a house-rent party. I wrote lots of poems about house-rent parties, and ate many a fried fish and pig's foot—with

Many Harlem residents gathered at after-hours clubs like this one that catered to blacks who were barred from high-end venues like the Cotton Club.

liquid refreshments on the side. I met ladies' maids and truck drivers, laundry workers and shoe shine boys, seamstresses and porters. I can still hear their laughter in my ears, hear the soft slow music, and feel the floor shaking as the dancers danced.[45]

For many Harlemites, rent parties were an opportunity to relax, out of the sight of disapproving relatives or neighbors. Of course they served not only a social but also a practical purpose because the tenant paid the rent with the profits earned from the party.

Stage Shows

In addition to the music performed in Harlem's clubs and other venues, there were plenty of theatrical performances to be found. Indeed, some of the first mainstream recognition of black entertainers and black culture came from white visitors attending musical revues, vaudeville acts, and plays. In fact, for black theater 1917 is considered by some to be the birth of the Harlem Renaissance because of the staging that year of Ridgley Torrence's *Three Plays for a Negro Theater*, which James Weldon Johnson

Josephine Baker, Renaissance Export

Of all the African American stage dancers who became famous during the Harlem Renaissance, few became as much of a celebrity as Josephine Baker. As Steven Watson writes in *The Harlem Renaissance*, though Baker's career began humbly, her comic style made her famous in Europe, where she became one of the renaissance's most beloved exports.

In 1920s Paris, Baker reigned as queen of "le jazz hot." To Europeans the star of the Revue Nègre and the Follies Bergère represented the high-voltage comic energy and primitive passion thought to characterize the Negro race. Although she seemed to achieve stardom overnight, she had been rejected early on at American auditions . . . because she was small, skinny, and unacceptably dark. Beginning at age thirteen, Baker worked as a dresser for traveling shows before being elevated to the chorus line. Clowning, dancing out of step, arms akimbo and eyes bugged out, she drew sufficient attention that she was dubbed "that comedy chorus girl" . . . but in her New York performances she remained in the chorus line. In 1925 she moved to France to appear in the Revue Nègre. Making her entrance upside down on the shoulders of a large black man, dressed only in a pink flamingo feather between her legs, she was an immediate sensation. Parisians embraced her comic, loose-limbed style and imbued her with their romantically primitivizing conception of blacks. On seeing Baker, art dealer Paul Guillame, for example, was prompted to write: "We who think we have a soul will blush at the poverty of our spiritual state before the superiority of blacks who have four souls, one in the head, one in the nose and throat, the shadow, and one in the blood."

Josephine Baker enjoyed tremendous success as a performer in Europe, where racist attitudes did not impede her rise to fame.

considered "the most important single event in the entire history of the Negro in the American Theater."[46] Although Torrence was white, his play was the first to feature blacks playing serious, positive roles.

In the early 1920s, *Shuffle Along*, written by the prolific songwriting duo of Eubie Blake and Noble Sissle, became the first musical revue to be created and performed entirely by blacks. It was very popular and spawned numerous other black-themed revues.

While at first many plays, revues, and musicals were written and performed by whites, the shows of the 1920s produced a host of African American actors, musicians, dancers, and singers. These individuals became celebrities in the 1920s, and many of them achieved lasting fame. Among them were Paul Robeson, Josephine Baker, John Bubbles, Adelaide Hall, Alberta Hunter, Nora Holt, Florence Mills, Bill "Bojangles" Robinson, Earl "Snakehips" Tucker, and others.

Music

Whether it was the jazz played in the high-end nightclubs, dance halls, cabarets, and revues, or the blues of the rent parties, gin mills, and speakeasies catering to the working class, music was an omnipresent, continuous soundtrack in Harlem.

The African American music genres of blues and jazz—which was at first known as ragtime—are rooted in black cultural history and experience. African rhythms, slave work songs, and spirituals all influenced the music heard in Harlem in the 1920s. This music, heard throughout the community, was central to the Harlem Renaissance. Floyd notes that aside from its entertainment value, the music of the period had a symbiotic relationship with the artistic movement:

> Music's role was . . . basic and important to the movement. . . . The idea that black music was America's only distinctive contribution to American and world musical culture was accepted and emphasized by Renaissance leaders and by some of the rank and file. . . . The Harlem Renaissance used and was supported and accompanied by music. The music of the black theater shows, the dance music of the cabarets, the blues and ragtime of the speakeasies and the

Bessie Smith's blues stylings made her famous during the Harlem Renaissance, and her recordings helped popularize blues music.

rent parties, the spirituals and the art songs of the recital and concert halls all created an ambiance for Renaissance activity and contemplation.[47]

The music of the Harlem Renaissance and those who performed it would leave a lasting mark on American culture. During this period, some of the twentieth century's most renowned figures in music began their careers in nightclubs and speakeasies. Among them were Bessie Smith, Ma Rainey, Fats Waller, Mamie Smith, Clara Smith, Duke Ellington, Louis Armstrong, W.C. Handy, and Fletcher Henderson. These musicians attracted the attention of record companies. The records they made reached an even wider audience and helped spread the music throughout the country and across the Atlantic into Europe.

The African-inspired rhythms of jazz spawned many dance crazes. Here, a couple of Harlem club goers perform the jitterbug on the dance floor of the Savoy.

Scholars say that the music these and other musicians performed is among the most significant elements of the period. In fact, so central was jazz to the Harlem Renaissance that the period is even popularly known as the Jazz Age.

The musicians of the Harlem Renaissance, however, had an influence that transcended their unique art form. They helped create an entire American subculture of language and dress that influenced the 1920s generation and those that came afterward. Black culture scholar Bruce M. Tyler writes:

The . . . [music] world in the 1920s produced a highly sophisticated subculture with its own language and dress codes that filtered increasingly into the general population of whites and blacks. Black society usually was the first to accept the trends, and "hep" whites, usually those in the entertainment world, soon followed, bringing along white party-goers who also participated in the jive and jazz culture.[48]

Dance Halls

The energetic black music helped create and was accompanied by an unprecedented dance craze in America. Until the 1920s, most American forms of dance were restricted to those performed in the traditional ballroom setting; however, the new music inspired what would become known as "jazz dance" or "modern dance." Like jazz and blues themselves, jazz dances were indigenous to America but were still the result of the crossbreeding of African rhythms and dances, European jigs, and minstrel show routines. Popular dances established by African Americans included the turkey trot, the shim sham, the boogie-woogie, the shag, and others. Additionally, jazz inspired white dancers to improvise steps of their own, including the Charleston and the Lindy Hop.

Thanks to the music performed there during the era, Harlem became a preferred destination for young adults eager to dance. Among the Harlem dance halls, the Alhambra and the Savoy Ballroom were the most popular and well known. The Savoy, known as "the Home of Happy Feet," was a block-long building on Lenox Avenue between 140th and 141st streets. The enormous interiors were adorned with chandeliers and marble steps. Up to four thousand people could dance through the night on the burnished maple floor as the best jazz orchestras in the city played. The Savoy was renowned and was the venue where many of the dances of the era gained popularity. The Savoy was also racially democratic, at least while the music was playing, as blacks and whites mingled on the dance floor.

Parties, Salons, and Social Life

The social scene of Harlem was not limited to the clubs, dance halls, cabarets, and speakeasies. Gatherings and parties were crucial to the renaissance's artistic community. Meetings and dinners attended by wealthy socialites, philanthropists, and others were held at the Civic Club, and literary and intellectual talks were frequently held in the homes of the Talented Tenth. However, among the most significant social networking occurred at the lavish parties thrown by figures such as A'Lelia Walker.

Although A'Lelia Walker's grandparents had been poor sharecroppers, her mother, Madame C.J. Walker, had parlayed profits from a chain of beauty salons into a fortune in real estate. A'Lelia Walker inherited this fortune and moved to Harlem in the early 1920s. There she became renowned as a hostess, throwing parties at one or the other of her mansions, one in Irvington and the other in Harlem. Then, in 1928 Walker announced that she was interested in promoting the cultural life of Harlem. She opened a salon–tea room called the Dark Tower, a reference to the column written by poet Countee Cullen in *Opportunity*.

Parties like those at Walker's Dark Tower were sumptuous affairs where wealthy people interested in the arts but from otherwise vastly different backgrounds mingled. According to Cary Wintz,

> Her parties were attended by English Rothschilds, French princesses, Russian grand dukes, members of the New York social register and stock exchange, Harlem luminaries, Prohibition and gambling nobility, and a fair number of nattily attired employees of the U.S. Postal Office and the Pullman Corporation.[49]

Such social mixing was important not only because it served as a venue for the exchange of ideas but because it provided opportunities for black literary figures to meet potential patrons.

The Scene

■

Harlem during the 1920s was a lively venue for art, entertainment, and intellectuals. In his essay "Home to Harlem," which appears in the Studio Museum in Harlem's publication, *Harlem Renaissance Art of Black America*, David Leverling Lewis describes the rich landscape of activity available to residents and visitors.

Almost everything seemed possible above 125th Street in the early 1920s. . . . The variety of things to do and see seemed enormous. There were the exhilarating Garveyite rallies at Liberty Hall. . . . At the 135th Street YMCA, Columbia's John Dewey or . . . [W.E.B.] DuBois might be speaking. . . .

Dramatic productions at the "Y" were major happenings . . . The intellectual pulse of Harlem was most accurately taken at the 135th Street branch of The New York Public Library . . . for there at evening readings of poetry, novels, and plays, the community's novices often received their first and most revealing assessments. . . .

Just off Lenox Avenue, eight blocks above the library, was Arthur "Happy" Rhone's club. Happy Rhone was the first black club owner to hire waitresses and the first to present floor shows in his plush establishment. . . . In the Jungle (that is, 133rd Street) there was Pod's and Jerry's (The Catagonia Club), along with Banks's Basement Brownie's, The Bucket of Blood, and . . . Leroy's—places beyond the pale for "respectable" Harlemites. Barton's was for the Whites and the small but celebrated Black sporting crowd. . . . To Harlem's aficionados the best clubs were the ones few downtown Whites knew about. . . .

Saturday nights were terrific in Harlem. . . . After the sedate parlor gathering and after the cabarets closed down, poets and writers . . . often would follow musicians to one of the nightly rent-paying [parties].

Less stylish but no less important gatherings took place at Niggerati Manor. As the residence of many of the most experimental black writers and artists of the period, including Langston Hughes, Zora Neale Hurston, Wallace Thurman, Aaron Douglas, and Richard Bruce Nugent, Niggerati Manor was a place where artistic people met informally to talk, strategize about creative projects, and generally have a good time. The parties and happenings at Niggerati Manor were replete with bootleg liquor, marijuana, and other drugs. One visitor recalled:

> The story goes out that the bathtubs in the house were always packed with sourmash [the raw material for distilling alcohol], while gin flowed from all water taps and the flush boxes were filled with needle beer [non-alcoholic beer with alcohol added, often using a syringe]. . . . It was also said that the inmates of the house spent wild nights . . . and delirious days fleeing from pink elephants [alcohol-induced hallucinations].[50]

To many, the excesses of the nightlife suggested by the goings-on at places such as Niggerati Manor were very much a part of the appeal of Harlem. The phenomenon of Harlemania was complementary to the bohemian lifestyle affected by many young adults of the 1920s.

Despite the divisions of Harlem between the worlds of the elite and the common folk, the black and the white, the cultural flowering of the Harlem Renaissance and its various arts touched and influenced every Harlem resident and visitor. Harlemania was a fleeting phenomenon, lasting less than a decade, but it transformed Harlem and influenced American and European culture, leaving a legacy for history.

Chapter Five

Decline

The writers, artists, and musicians of the Harlem Renaissance were at their peak of popularity and productivity when, in October 1929, the U.S. stock market crashed. The crash set off a worldwide economic decline known as the Great Depression, which came to affect nearly every aspect of life in the United States. Though many factors have to be considered with regard to the end of the Harlem Renaissance, the stock market crash and the Great Depression that followed certainly loom large. Between October 1929 and the first Harlem race riot in 1935, which many historians consider the final death knell for the renaissance, the economic, social, and artistic vitality of Harlem gradually collapsed.

Fruit of the Renaissance

The success of African American writers, artists, musicians, and thinkers during the Harlem Renaissance gave blacks throughout America reason to hope that life was improving for them. The 1920s was a period of general economic growth in the United States, and although few African Americans shared in the increased wealth in a measure commensurate to their population, there was a nearly 70 percent growth in the black middle class and a significant increase in the black ownership of businesses and the number of blacks making a living in business. One measure of the rising prosperity was the increase in the

In 1922 a large group of African Americans marches in Washington, D.C., with signs condemning the continued practice of lynching in the United States.

number of black real estate brokers and the fact that almost every major northern city had a black-owned bank.

Black Americans achieved several important legal victories during the 1920s as well. Among these were judicial decisions in lawsuits filed by the NAACP against discrimination and institutionalized racism in the government, including the criminal justice system. For example, in 1926 civil rights lawyers pursued and won the acquittal of a black man who, along with his brothers, had opened fire on a white mob while defending his house, which he had purchased in a white neighborhood.

In addition to pressing for civil rights, the New Negro movement, with its strong emphasis on education, saw success in the form of a sixfold increase in the number of African American college graduates between 1917 and 1927. This trend produced growth in the black middle class and laid the foundation for an increase in the number of blacks in professions such as medicine, law, and dentistry. The NAACP also played a role in this growth by suing Harlem Hospital for discriminating against blacks in hiring staff members. The staff had been all white, but by 1925 there were five black doctors working at the hospital and a school to train black nurses was planned.

However, most of these economic and social gains made during the Harlem Renaissance proved to be temporary. The economic downturn that followed the stock market crash of 1929 eventually ravaged Harlem. Cary D. Wintz notes that Harlem, once a symbol of hope, during the Depression became for many a symbol of despair:

> Harlem, then, symbolized different things to different blacks. It was both their hope and their despair. . . . It was a symbol of the black migrant who left the South and went north with dreams of freedom and opportunity. It also symbolized the shattered pieces of those dreams which lay half-buried beneath the filth and garbage of the city slum. Harlem reflected the self-confidence, militancy, and pride of the New Negro in his or her demand for equality; it reflected the aspirations and genius of the writers and poets of the Harlem Renaissance; but Harlem, like the black migrant, like the New Negro, and like the Renaissance writers, did not resolve its problems or fulfill its dreams. Everything, it seemed, fell short of its goal.[51]

Optimism

Despite the stock market crash, many Harlem Renaissance figures maintained their optimism in the first few years of the Great Depression, and in fact, it seemed for a time that the renaissance was going stronger than ever. Harlem remained the cultural center of black America. Many of the renaissance writers were still active and getting published, and the economy of Harlem appeared to be maintaining itself: The rich still patronized the uptown clubs, and the speakeasies, dance halls, and theaters did great business catering to those who could still afford to patronize them.

In 1930 Harlem Renaissance elder James Weldon Johnson, in his book *Black Manhattan*, expressed the optimism and hope that many in Harlem retained. In this book, Johnson details the history of African Americans in Manhattan and, while recognizing the potential for racial conflict as the white and black populations increased, he praises the progress made in race relations and looks toward a bright future for all of New York, particularly for Harlem. He wrote, "The Negro's situation in Harlem is without precedent in all his history in New York; never before has he been so securely anchored, never before has he owned the land, never before has he had so well established a community life."[52]

Ghetto to Slum

However, economic conditions across the nation continued to worsen and there was no immediate end in sight to the Depression. Between 1931 and 1935, as the economy worsened, the outlook for most Americans deteriorated. For African Americans, including those few who had amassed any kind of wealth, prospects declined even more rapidly than they did for whites. Harlem's black economy, events proved, was far more fragile than anyone had realized. In part this was because Harlem had never been home to substantial numbers of middle-class blacks but instead to large numbers of poor and working-class people living paycheck to paycheck.

The relatively small black middle class had some money in black-owned banks, but as these institutions collapsed all over the country, black businesses went under, and the fortunes of the middle class drained away. Even the champion of the Talented Tenth, W.E.B. DuBois, lost his home and life insurance.

Adding to Harlem's problems was a huge increase in residents, most of them poor. Even at the height of its renaissance, Harlem had many poor residents. Through much of the 1920s Harlem had also been burdened with overcrowding, as new residents arrived. Many of the new migrants to Harlem were poor blacks who had left the South. The combination of poverty and overcrowding turned Harlem into a slum. According to Harlem scholar Gilbert Osofsky,

> The most profound change that Harlem experienced in the 1920s was its emergence as a slum. Largely within the

End of the Renaissance Makers

───────────■───────────

"The Harlem Renaissance died as the people who created it ceased to exist," writes Cary D. Wintz in *Black Culture and the Harlem Renaissance*. In the following excerpt, Wintz describes the fate of several key figures who were vital to the literary movement of the period.

In 1931 Madam A'Lelia Walker died, and the dream of establishing a Harlem literary salon died with her. Three years later Wallace Thurman and [novelist] Rudolph Fisher were also dead. Before the end of the decade James Weldon Johnson was killed in an automobile accident. Claude McKay and Countee Cullen survived into the mid 1940s, but in the last ten years of their lives they produced little of literary value. . . . Other Renaissance writers suffered an even sadder fate. Nella Larsen, Jean Toomer, and Zora Neale Hurston simply faded into obscurity. Hurston's last years were particularly indicative of how far these writers had fallen from the celebrity status that they had enjoyed when Harlem was in vogue. Hurston, short of money, and all but forgotten, spent the last years of her life working as a maid in Florida. In 1959 she suffered a stroke; a year later she died in a welfare home and was buried in an unmarked grave in a segregated cemetery.

space of a single decade, Harlem was transformed from a potentially ideal community to a neighborhood with manifold social and economic problems called "deplorable, unspeakable, incredible."[53]

The population problem only worsened in the 1930s as poor blacks continued to move to Harlem even as its economy collapsed. The swelling of Harlem's population led to a host of other troubles, including extreme housing shortages and high rents, high unemployment, and the breakdown of the family due to the

The Harlem Riot

For many, the 1935 Harlem race riot marked the end of the Harlem Renaissance. The following account of the riot is excerpted from the History of Jim Crow Web site.

Rioting broke out in the Harlem section of New York City on March 19, 1935, after an African-American youth was alleged to have stolen a knife from a store on 125th Street. The young suspect was not apprehended but rumors spread in the black community that he had been beaten and killed by police. These rumors, coupled with charges of police brutality and merchant employment discrimination, triggered rioting by African Americans in Harlem. At least six hundred store windows were shattered and looting was rampant. The riot resulted in the deaths of three blacks and caused over $200 million worth of property damage. Police arrested seventy-five people, mostly blacks, and nearly sixty citizens were seriously injured.

A Harlem resident surveys the damage to a local shop after the 1935 riot. The violence signaled the end of Harlem as a cultural hotspot.

necessity of many men leaving their families behind as they searched for work elsewhere. Preventable health problems increased as over-crowding grew worse and people had less money than usual to pay for visits to doctors. Furthermore, all these social factors contributed to increases in drug abuse and crime.

The housing shortage was exploited by landlords and developers who subdivided existing buildings and built cheap tenement buildings. Despite the dilapidated condition of most dwellings, black tenants were forced to pay between $10 and $30 more per month in rent than whites, representing on average twice the percentage of their incomes. Rents were so high that many people were forced to share space with other tenants, often using the so-called hot-bed system in which a bed would be shared by two different people who worked and slept in shifts opposite each other.

Economic and Social Decline

Despite the initial apparent hardiness of Harlem's entertainment industry, the Depression was particularly lethal for the businesses that were part of the Harlem nightlife. Clubs, dance halls, and theaters closed as their financial backers went broke or pulled out in search of better investments. Harlem suffered a major blow in 1933 when the ratification of the Twenty-first Amendment to the Constitution put an end to Prohibition. Without the draw and money generated by illegal alcohol sales, the uptown nightclubs died out quickly due to competition from new establishments in downtown Manhattan. The dollars of white revelers as well as many of the talented black entertainers who had worked in the venues quickly disappeared from Harlem.

Other businesses fared poorly as well. Although Harlem had attracted a large number of intellectuals and artists and was home to black institutions such as churches, civil rights organizations, and newspapers, it had relatively few black-owned businesses. Blacks owned less than 20 percent of Harlem's approximately 10,000 businesses. Despite making up a population of about 225,000 in Manhattan, blacks owned only 258 businesses, which was fewer than many other cities with a fraction of the black population. Furthermore, black-owned stores were small, employing only one or two people, so what black entrepreneurship did exist had little effect on the unemployment problem. For most Harlem residents, low income and high unemployment became ever more prevalent during the 1930s. The median income dropped 43 percent in the first years of the Depression; by 1935, 50 percent of Harlem was unemployed.

As jobs became scarcer, racial discrimination in employment rose. As more and more whites lost higher-paying jobs, they began to take the menial and service jobs traditionally held by blacks. In an era when discrimination in hiring was perfectly legal, many employers chose white applicants whenever they were available. Despite the fact that Harlem was predominantly black, job discrimination was routinely practiced there. Even during the 1920s, few retail establishments—even those that relied on black customers for their business—hired blacks at all, and if they did it was usually only for menial work such as janitorial duties.

At the same time, educational discrimination made it difficult for blacks to qualify for jobs that were available. Vocational schools often refused to train blacks in certain fields, such as office work and skilled labor. Public school districts were manipulated to segregate black students in schools that were underfunded and that offered a curriculum that assured little opportunity for advancement beyond the lowest-paying jobs.

These factors led to dire social problems in Harlem during the 1930s. Because of high unemployment, many men had to look for work in other cities or towns, causing an increase in households where the father was absent. Most families lived in poverty, and Harlem emerged as the city's leader in crime and drug addiction.

Health deteriorated for most black Harlem residents. Hospitals were overcrowded as a result. Rates of preventable diseases such as syphilis and tuberculosis rose many times higher than they did for whites. The mortality rates for black adults and infants were the highest in New York City.

Little Recourse

Despite the significant victories of the NAACP, blacks had little political recourse to help themselves out of the dismal situation in Harlem. Political power remained in the hands of whites. Although elsewhere there were a handful of African American politicians at the state and local levels, Harlem was part of a congressional district that included immigrants from Eastern Europe, Ireland, and Italy. As a result, no black candidate was able to assemble the votes to be elected to Congress.

Furthermore, national politics were in a state of upheaval during the early 1930s. The Republican Party, the party of Abraham

In this 1936 photo, a restaurant owner stands in the doorway as he waits for customers. Throughout the 1930s, few Harlem families could afford such luxuries as eating out.

Lincoln, who had been responsible for emancipation, had dominated the White House and been supported by most African Americans since Reconstruction. However, in the face of the sustained economic calamity of the Great Depression, in the 1932 elections the party lost most of its African American votes to Democratic candidate Franklin Delano Roosevelt (FDR), whose policies promised to turn around the economy as well as to improve conditions for blacks. However, FDR and his fellow moderates and liberals never could overcome the strength of southern Democrats, who blocked many efforts to help alleviate the suffering in poor black communities like Harlem.

Franklin D. Roosevelt was the first Democrat to have the support of black voters. His policies, however, were often thwarted by the racist beliefs of southern Democrats.

Economic Effect on the Arts

No single aspect explains the decline of the Harlem Renaissance. This is in part why scholars have difficulty assigning an exact date to the end of the movement. Still, there is no doubt that the literary and artistic life of Harlem was undermined by the Depression.

Others, however, argue that the Harlem Renaissance was claimed by problems unrelated to economics. As early as 1931, Alain Locke had voiced doubts about the longevity of the Harlem Renaissance, suggesting that somehow the quality of the artistic product had suffered as quantity increased:

> The much exploited Negro renaissance was after all a product of the expansive period we are now willing to call the period of inflation and overproduction; perhaps there was much in it that was unsound, and perhaps our aesthetic

Change of Heart

W.E.B. DuBois had been a proponent of assimilation; however, in the mid-1930s, when black institutions were suffering financially, he reevaluated his position. In this 1934 essay, reprinted in Theodore G. Vincent's *Voices of a Black Nation*, DuBois draws a distinction between white-imposed segregation and voluntary separation, arguing in favor of the latter. This break from NAACP philosophy led to DuBois's leaving the organization in 1934.

> The experience in the United States has been that usually when there is racial segregation, there is also racial discrimination.
>
> But the two things do not necessarily go together. . . . Not only is there no objection to colored people living beside colored people if the surroundings and treatment involve no discrimination, if [conditions are good, there can be no objection]. . . .
>
> It must be remembered that in the last quarter of a century, the advance of the colored people has been mainly in the lines where they themselves, working by and for themselves, have accomplished the greatest advances. . . .
>
> There is no doubt that numbers of white people . . . stand ready to take the most distinct advantage of voluntary segregation and cooperation among colored people [and use it] as a point of attack and discrimination. Our counter attack should be, therefore, against discrimination. . . . But never in the world should our fight be against association with ourselves because by that very token we give up the whole argument that we are worth associating with.

gods are turning their backs only a little more gracefully than the gods of the marketplace. Are we then in a period of cultural depression, verging on spiritual bankruptcy? . . . Are we outliving the Negro fad? . . . Yes.[54]

In addition, the Depression made it harder for the few black writers and artists who were managing to support themselves to continue doing so. As a result of the hard times, most of the Harlem Renaissance writers experienced continual money problems, and most were in debt. Many relied on Negrotarian patronage, which to a great extent evaporated during the Depression. Additionally, with leaner budgets, the *Crisis* and *Opportunity* published less and less literature in their pages. The literary award events became more sporadic and eventually stopped altogether for lack of interest and funds.

Defections and Dispersal

The artistic decline was gradual. Infighting, the loss of donors, interpersonal disputes, and the deaths of some Renaissance figures dissolved many connections within the movement. Although there was no mass exodus of writers and artists, one by one they dropped away. Many left to pursue opportunities elsewhere; others left because they became disillusioned with the direction of the movement or because they considered it to be in decline and wished to leave before the bitter end. At the same time, Harlem stopped attracting newcomers, and up-and-coming black writers and artists elected not to associate their work with that of the Harlem Renaissance establishment.

Even before the Wall Street crash, the dispersal of many of the Talented Tenth founders and their protégés had begun. Charles S. Johnson left his post at *Opportunity* in 1928 to teach at Fisk University in Nashville. He was followed by James Weldon Johnson in 1931 and artist Aaron Douglas in 1937, both of whom also went to Fisk.

Jessie Fauset gave up her position at the *Crisis* in 1926 to write. She married in 1929 and then also gave up her writing, publishing her last book in 1933. Alain Locke returned to Washington, D.C., and Howard University in the early 1930s.

Even W.E.B. DuBois left the NAACP and the *Crisis* in 1934 over a dispute regarding a change in his political philosophy. A longtime advocate of assimilation, DuBois was forced to leave when he began supporting what he called "voluntary (by blacks) segregation." DuBois believed correctly that the economic downturn caused by the worldwide depression would be harder on blacks than whites. However, his new position that voluntary separation between the races would somehow ensure economic survival of the race was not accepted by many, including his closest associates in the Talented Tenth.

Deaths and Disputes

The Harlem Renaissance also lost several of its important figures to death. One of the most notable was the untimely death of beautician-philanthropist A'Lelia Walker, an important supporter of black writers and artists. Walker, who had been planning to open a literary salon in Harlem, was financially destroyed by the Great Depression. Eight months after much of her business property was auctioned off, she died at age forty-six from heart trouble. Langston Hughes said her death was a sad landmark: "That was really the end of the gay times of the New Negro Era in Harlem."[55]

Three years later, in December 1934, the renaissance also lost Wallace Thurman, who, although he was only in his late twenties, died after a drinking binge from complications related to tuberculosis.

According to Steven Watson, however, just as much as these untimely deaths and defections, disputes among the Harlem Renaissance figures contributed to the ultimate downfall of the movement. He says that the "movement was . . . torn apart by internal contradictions (Niggerati versus Talented Tenth, politics versus art, race building versus literature)."[56]

In addition to the disagreements on how blacks should be portrayed or what the purpose of black art should be, personal fallings-out occurred among many of the figures during the 1920s and 1930s. For example, Langston Hughes and Zora Neale Hurston worked together on an idea for a folk opera titled *Mule Bone* from 1927 until 1930, with the financial backing of Negrotarian Charlotte Mason. The Hurston-Hughes-Mason combination had been among the most successful writer/patron relationships of the Harlem Renaissance. However, Alain Locke, who had been close to Hughes and Hurston for many years, reported to Mason that the two writers were not working hard enough on the project for which she was paying. In response, Mason cut off finances and contact with them. Hughes and Hurston were both upset by Locke and Mason's actions and the relationships soured. Hughes and Hurston later completed *Mule Bone*, but despite Hughes's contributions, Hurston copyrighted the work under her name alone, claiming full credit. Lingering resentment over Hurston's taking full credit finally led to the end of her relationship with Hughes.

Disillusioned and convinced that the renaissance was doomed due to economic factors, Hughes left the country in 1931, bound for Haiti and Cuba. "That spring," he later said, "for me (and I guess, all of us) was the end of the Harlem Renaissance."[57] Hughes left the States again in 1932 for Russia, where he was to work on a socialist film. Other than for short visits, he would not live in

The financial ruin and death of A'Lelia Walker (right), a major financial supporter of the Harlem Renaissance, helped bring about the end of the movement.

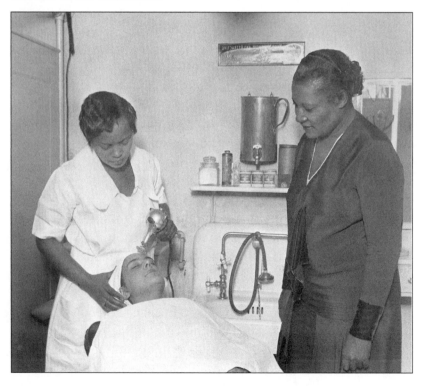

the United States for nearly ten years after that. Hughes was the only Harlem Renaissance writer to support himself on his art alone and had the longest and most successful career; thus his absence from the circle of writers in Harlem was a notable one.

A Last Gasp

In the early 1930s, the end of the Harlem Renaissance seemed imminent—if not already past—even to its founders. According to many critics, the Harlem Renaissance was too dependent on white money, white opinion, and white audiences to sustain itself independently and was destined to ultimately fail to deliver on the unrealistic social goals its founders had set. In 1934, upon leaving the *Crisis*, a disillusioned W.E.B. DuBois gave a similar assessment of the movement's decline:

> It was because it was a transplanted and exotic thing. It was a literature written for the benefit of white people and at the behest of white readers, and started out privately from the white point of view.[58]

However, though many said the renaissance was all but dead by 1933, those involved with the movement experienced one last burst of creative productivity and energy. During this period, over a dozen books by black writers were published.

In March 1935 a massive race riot broke out in Harlem after a black youth was arrested for theft and allegedly abused by white police officers. The incident touched off a riot in which three African Americans were killed. Many historians mark the riot as the end of the Harlem Renaissance.

However, even after the riot there was one final artistic push as Langston Hughes's play *Mulatto* opened in New York in October, becoming the first full-length play written by a black author to play on Broadway. Hughes was one of the few writers from the Harlem Renaissance who managed to survive it for more than a handful of years. Zora Neale Hurston, Nella Larsen, Countee Cullen, and others continued to write for a time, but most died within a few years of the renaissance's end or faded into obscurity, where they remained until scholars and other writers unearthed their works in the latter decades of the twentieth century.

Police round up looters during the Harlem race riot of 1935. Many historians identify the riot as the end of the Harlem Renaissance.

The music associated with the Harlem Renaissance, especially jazz, was far more robust in its staying power. Although the queen of the blues, Bessie Smith, died from injuries sustained in a car crash in Mississippi in 1937, many of the other musicians who gained fame in Harlem during the 1920s successfully continued their careers elsewhere. Several, such as Louis Armstrong, Duke Ellington, and Fletcher Henderson, went on to become legendary and highly influential entertainers, inspiring future generations of jazz artists. In the musical arena, then, the Harlem Renaissance lived on.

Epilogue

Legacy

Scholars continue to debate the legacy of the Harlem Renaissance. Even during the 1920s and 1930s, the influence of the Harlem Renaissance varied widely among the black population. Many of the books produced during the twenties and thirties were read by predominantly white audiences and had insignificant impact on most blacks. As Langston Hughes later claimed, the New Negro vogue little altered the day-to-day life of average blacks, most of whom were too poor to buy the books written by the renaissance figures: "The ordinary Negroes hadn't heard of the Negro Renaissance. And if they had, it hadn't raised their wages any."[59]

Furthermore, the hopes of the founders of the renaissance that literature could serve as a means to end discrimination and aid assimilation were not realized. Even the popularity of black writing, black writers, and the music and art of Harlem did little to cause the majority of whites to reconsider their racial prejudices.

According to most critics, along with the penetration of black music into mainstream culture—on which much of American rock music is founded—the most significant impact the Harlem Renaissance made was on the future generations of black writers and artists. These include writers such as James Baldwin, Gwendolyn Brooks, Amiri Baraka, William Attaway, Ralph Ellison, Margaret Walker, Richard Wright, and Frank Yerby as well as artists Romare Bearden, Charles White, Jacob Lawrence, and Charles Sebree. Many of these figures learned about the Harlem Renaissance through school or through immersing themselves in the music of the period.

The Harlem Renaissance was considered by most to be a failure as a social movement. Most of its literary figures faded into obscurity for many years, and some critics go so far as to claim that no masterpieces of American literature were produced during that time. However, according to some scholars, the movement was a success because more black writers wrote and published more work than ever before in American history. Furthermore, simply by bringing the black experience to the consciousness of white America, the writers made a significant contribution. According to poet Amiri Baraka (writing as LeRoi Jones), particularly momentous were rebels such as Hughes who dared to write about the experience of poor blacks even though it upset the Talented Tenth critics. Baraka applauded them for writing "literature about poverty, a literature about violence, a literature about the seamier side of the so-called American Dream."[60]

The Harlem Renaissance was a relatively brief social and artistic movement, cut short by world economic circumstances as well as flaws and fragilities within itself. Despite being short-lived, it left its mark on American culture, as well as the cultures into which it was exported, such as Europe and parts of Africa.

In addition, many involved in the civil rights struggles of the mid- to late twentieth century and early twenty-first century found inspiration in the writings, the art, and the music of the New Negro movement and the Harlem Renaissance. Many looked—and still look—to the writings of figures such as DuBois, McKay, Hughes, and others for insight and encouragement.

Finally, although the writing, the art, and the music itself is of the past, in the decades since, many writers, artists, scholars, and others of all races have been inspired by the hope and desire that launched the movement and in the optimistic belief that progress, equality, and justice might be advanced by the arts.

Notes

Introduction:
Harlem, City of Hope

1. Alain Locke, ed., *The New Negro: An Interpretation*. New York: Albert and Charles Boni, 1925, p. 6.
2. Steven Watson, *The Harlem Renaissance: Hub of African-American Culture, 1920–1930*. New York: Pantheon, 1995, p. 13.
3. *New York Dispatch*, "The Hope and Promise of Harlem," January 7, 1921, quoted in Theodore G. Vincent, ed., *Voices of a Black Nation*. San Francisco: Ramparts, 1973, pp. 75–76

Chapter 1:
The "New Negro" Movement

4. W.E.B. DuBois, *The Souls of Black Folk*. New York: Modern Library, 2003, pp. xli, 42.
5. Quoted in Watson, *The Harlem Renaissance*, p.17.
6. Cary D. Wintz, *Black Culture and the Harlem Renaissance*. Houston: Rice University Press, 1988, pp. 11–12.
7. W.E.B. DuBois, "Returning Soldiers," *Crisis*, May 1919, quoted in Vincent, Voices of a Black Nation, p. 80.
8. David Leverling Lewis, *When Harlem Was in Vogue*. New York: Penguin, 1997, p. xxv.
9. Cyril V. Briggs, "The Old Negro Goes: Let Him Go in Peace," *Crusader*, October 1919, quoted in Vincent, *Voices of a Black Nation*, p. 64.
10. George S. Schuyler, "The Integrationist Vision," *Pittsburgh Courier*, June 11, 1927, quoted in Vincent, *Voices of a Black Nation*, p. 70.
11. Quoted in *The Rise and Fall of Jim Crow*, Quest Productions, VideoLine Productions, and Thirteen/WNET New York, 2002.
12. Quoted in Watson, *The Harlem Renaissance*, p. 19.
13. W.E.B. DuBois, "Marcus Garvey: A Lunatic or a Traitor?" *Crisis*, May 1924, quoted in Vincent, *Voices of a Black Nation*, p. 105.
14. Marcus Garvey, "What Garvey Thinks of DuBois," *Negro World*, January 13, 1923, quoted in Vincent, *Voices of a Black Nation*, p. 97.
15. Wintz, *Black Culture and the Harlem Renaissance*, p. 31.

Chapter 2:
Ushering in the Renaissance

16. Wintz, *Black Culture and the Harlem Renaissance*, p. 63.
17. Quoted in Studio Museum in Harlem, *Harlem Renaissance Art of Black America*. New York: Abradale, 1987, p. 62.
18. David Leverling Lewis, ed., *The Harlem Renaissance Reader*. New

York: Viking, 1994, p. xix.

19. Lewis, *The Harlem Renaissance Reader*, pp. xxv–xxvi.

20. Quoted in Watson, *The Harlem Renaissance*, p. 19.

21. Quoted in Vincent, *Voices of a Black Nation*, p. 50.

22. Lewis, *The Harlem Renaissance Reader*, pp. xxv–xxvi.

23. Quoted in Watson, *The Harlem Renaissance*, p. 26.

24. Quoted in Lewis, *When Harlem Was in Vogue*, p. 125.

25. Lewis, *When Harlem Was in Vogue*, p. 51.

Chapter 3:
Voices of the Harlem Renaissance

26. Quoted in "Jessie Redman Fauset," The Black Renaissance in Washington, D.C., 1920–1930s, June 20, 2003. www.dclibrary.org/blkren/bios/fausetjr.html.

27. Locke, *The New Negro*, pp.8–9.

28. DuBois, *The Souls of Black Folk*, pp. 5–6.

29. Nathan Irvin Huggins, ed., *Voices from the Harlem Renaissance*. New York: Oxford University Press, 1995, p. 135.

30. Quoted in Lewis, *When Harlem Was in Vogue*, p. 193.

31. Watson, *The Harlem Renaissance*, p. 91.

32. Quoted in the Studio Museum in Harlem, *Harlem Renaissance Art of Black America*, p. 71.

33. Lewis, *The Harlem Renaissance Reader*, p. xxxii.

34. Quoted in J. Martin Favor, *Authentic Blackness*. Durham NC: Duke University Press, 1999, p. 9.

35. Langston Hughes, "The Negro Artist and the Racial Mountain," *Nation,* June 23, 1926, p. 2.

36. Marcus Garvey, "'Home to Harlem': An Insult to the Race," *Negro World,* September 28, 1928, quoted in Vincent, *Voices of a Black Nation*, p. 357.

37. Quoted in Lewis, *When Harlem Was in Vogue*, p. 225.

38. Wintz, *Black Culture and the Harlem Renaissance*, p. 95.

Chapter 4: Harlemania

39. Wintz, *Black Culture and the Harlem Renaissance*, p. 94.

40. Wintz, *Black Culture and the Harlem Renaissance*, pp. 88, 92.

41. Lewis, *When Harlem Was in Vogue*, p. 157.

42. Samuel A. Floyd Jr., ed., *Black Music in the Harlem Renaissance*. Knoxville: University of Tennessee Press, 1990, p. 3.

43. Quoted in Lewis, *When Harlem Was in Vogue*, p. 208.

44. Watson, *The Harlem Renaissance*, p. 128.

45. Quoted in Wintz, *Black Culture and the Harlem Renaissance*, p. 92.

46. Quoted in Geneviève Fabre and Michel Feith, eds., *Temples for Tomorrow: Looking Back at the Harlem Renaissance*. Bloomington: Indiana University Press, 2001, p. 35.

47. Floyd, *Black Music in the Harlem Renaissance*, p. 3.

48. Bruce M. Tyler, *From Harlem to Hollywood: The Struggle for Racial and*

Cultural Democracy, 1920–1943. New York: Garland, 1992, p. 199.

49. Quoted in Wintz, *Black Culture and the Harlem Renaissance*, p. 91.
50. Quoted in Watson, *The Harlem Renaissance*, p. 89.

Chapter 5: Decline

51. Wintz, *Black Culture and the Harlem Renaissance*, pp. 28–29.
52. Quoted in Huggins, *Voices from the Harlem Renaissance*, p. 71.
53. Quoted in Wintz, *Black Culture and the Harlem Renaissance*, p. 24.
54. Quoted in Wintz, *Black Culture and the Harlem Renaissance*, p. 223.
55. Quoted in Watson, *The Harlem Renaissance*, p. 165.
56. Watson, *The Harlem Renaissance*, p. 159.
57. Quoted in Lewis, *When Harlem Was in Vogue*, p. 261.
58. Quoted in Watson, *The Harlem Renaissance*, p. 159.

Epilogue: Legacy

59. Quoted in Wintz, *Black Culture and the Harlem Renaissance.* p. 225.
60. Quoted in Wintz, *Black Culture and the Harlem Renaissance*, p. 228.

For Further Reading

Books

Emily Bernard, ed., *Remember Me to Harlem: The Letters of Langston Hughes and Carl Van Vechten, 1925–1964.* New York: Alfred A. Knopf, 2001. A collection of correspondence between Harlem Renaissance writer Langston Hughes and "Negrotarian" writer Carl Van Vechten sent over the course of their long friendship. Includes photographs and some historic annotations by the editor.

Philip S. Bryant, *Zora Neale Hurston.* Chicago: Raintree, 2003. This short biography follows the life of anthropologist and writer Zora Neale Hurston, the best-known female member of the Harlem Renaissance. Includes a glossary, timeline, and bibliography of works focusing on Hurston's life. Also includes several black-and-white and color photographs.

Kerry Candaele, *Bound for Glory: Milestones in Black American History, 1910–1930.* Philadelphia: Chelsea House, 1997. Spanning the period from the massive northern migration of the beginning of the century through the 1930s Depression era, this book focuses on racial inequity, Pan-Africanism, the Harlem Renaissance, and the important figures of the period.

Seamus Cavan, *W.E.B. DuBois and Racial Relations.* Brookfield, CT: Millbrook, 1993. This brief history focuses on the race crisis of the early twentieth century and DuBois's contributions in combating racism. Includes a timeline of his life and several photographs.

Wayne F. Cooper, *Claude McKay: Rebel Sojourner in the Harlem Renaissance.* Baton Rouge: Louisiana State University Press, 1987. This biography of poet Claude McKay covers his life in depth, from birth to his death in 1948. Includes extensive notes and essays on source material.

Jessie Redmon Fauset, *There Is Confusion.* New York: Boni and Liveright, 1924. Considered the first novel of the Harlem Renaissance, this is Fauset's semiautobiographical portrayal of an educated and ambitious black family told from the perspective of a young, artistic black woman.

Langston Hughes, *The Langston Hughes Reader.* New York: George Brazillier, 1958. This collection of Hughes's writings includes short stories, poetry for adults and children, song lyrics, excerpts from novels, plays, articles, speeches, and autobiographical essays.

Geoffrey Jacques, *Free Within Ourselves: The Harlem Renaissance.* Danbury, CT: Franklin Watts, 1996. This history of the Harlem Renaissance includes chapters devoted to music, theater, literature, the visual arts, and other topics. Source notes and a nonannotated reading list are also provided.

Denise Jordan, *Harlem Renaissance Artists.* Chicago: Heinemann Library, 2003. This book provides biographies of eleven Harlem Renaissance visual artists, including photos of some of their work. Also contains a timeline and useful references to the artwork and books for further study.

Melissa McDaniel, *W.E.B. DuBois: Scholar and Civil Rights Activist.* New York: Grolier, 1999. This short biography of W.E.B. DuBois covers his life from birth to death, including a chronology, bibliography, and several black-and-white photographs.

Nellie Y. McKay, *Jean Toomer, Artist: A Study of His Literary Life and Work, 1894–1936.* This biography portrays the life of mixed-race writer Jean Toomer from his birth to his death, focusing on his literary accomplishments, the landmark *Cane* in particular. Includes a bibliography, suggested readings, and a few photographs.

Milton Meltzer, *Langston Hughes: An Illustrated Edition.* Brookfield, CT: Millbrook, 1997. This biography of Langston Hughes follows the writer's life from childhood to his death. Accompanying Meltzer's text are black-and-white drawings by Stephen Alcorn. Also included is a selected bibliography of Hughes's work and books on the writer.

Videos
Against the Odds: The Artists of the Harlem Renaissance. PBS Video, 1995. This documentary tells the struggle of black visual artists in the 1920s and 1930s to show and sell their work.

From These Roots: A Review of the Harlem Renaissance. Against the Odds/ William Greaves Productions, 1974. This video uses still photographs and filmed sequences to re-create the social and political climate of the Harlem Renaissance.

Hughes' Dream Harlem. New Heritage Films and D. Hutson LLC, 2002. This film shows how writer Langston Hughes successfully fused jazz, blues, and common speech to celebrate the beauty of black life during the Harlem Renaissance through spoken-word sessions, roundtable discussions, and a tour of Hughes's Harlem hangouts.

I remember Harlem. Films for the Humanities, 1981. This video traces the rise, decline, and regeneration of Harlem, America's largest black community, over three centuries.

Web Sites
Encyclopaedia Britannica's Guide to Black History (http://search.eb.com/ blackhistory). Covering eras in black history from the sixteenth century to the present, this site offers interactive menus to entries on people, places, institutions, organizations, terminology, and more. Also offers an extensive timeline of black history.

Harlem, 1900–1940
(www.si.umich.edu/CHICO/Harlem/index.html). This site from the Schomburg Center for Research in Black Culture offers biographies of Harlem Renaissance figures, histories, and photographs of African-American institutions and organizations in Harlem and New York. Also includes an interactive timeline reference link and a bibliography of books for adults and for young readers.

The History of Jim Crow (www.jimcrowhistory.org). This site, associated with the video series *The Rise and Fall of Jim Crow*, provides essays, history resources, a U.S. map depicting the use of Jim Crow laws, lesson plans, and other resources for students and teachers.

Works Consulted

Books

W.E.B. DuBois, *The Gift of Black Folk*. New York: AMS, 1971. A reprint of the 1924 edition of DuBois's collection of essays dealing with African American history, identity, culture, and politics.

————, *The Souls of Black Folk*. New York: Modern Library, 2003. A reprint of DuBois's seminal 1903 collection of essays in which he anticipated and helped establish the founding creed of the New Negro movement of the 1910s and 1920s.

Gerald Early, ed., *My Soul's High Songs: The Collected Writings of Countee Cullen, Voice of the Harlem Renaissance*. New York: Doubleday, 1991. This collection includes much of Cullen's poetry and prose. Also contains a lengthy introductory biography and analysis of his work by the editor.

Geneviève Fabre and Michel Feith, eds., *Temples for Tomorrow: Looking Back at the Harlem Renaissance*. Bloomington: Indiana University Press, 2001. A collection of scholarly essays on a variety of topics related to the history, art, and legacy of the Harlem Renaissance. Includes a subject-organized timeline of the Harlem Renaissance and the years surrounding it.

J. Martin Favor, *Authentic Blackness*. Durham, NC: Duke University Press, 1999. This book contains scholarly essays on some of the major works and themes of the Harlem Renaissance, relating them to their place in history and contemporary culture.

Samuel A. Floyd Jr., ed., *Black Music in the Harlem Renaissance*. Knoxville: University of Tennessee Press, 1990. This collection of essays on African American music deals with vocal concert music, musical theaters, the relationship of art to music, and the central nature of music to black life during the Harlem Renaissance.

Nikki Giovanni, *Shimmy Shimmy Shimmy Like My Sister Kate: Looking at the Harlem Renaissance Through Poems*. New York: Henry Holt, 1996. Includes poems by such authors as Paul Laurence Dunbar, Langston Hughes, and Countee Cullen, as well as contemporary poets influenced by them, such as Gwendolyn Brooks and Amiri Baraka (LeRoi Jones), with commentary and a discussion of the development of the Harlem Renaissance.

Nathan Irvin Huggins, ed., *Voices from the Harlem Renaissance*. New York: Oxford University Press, 1995. This collection contains more than 120 selections from some of the most important political and literary writing of the Harlem Renaissance, along with numerous plates showing paintings and sculptures by artists of the period.

Jackie Kay, *Bessie Smith*. Somerset, England: Absolute, 1997. This biography of blues queen Bessie Smith contains a detailed and sexually frank account of her life and career, including the period spent in Harlem during the renaissance.

————, *When Harlem Was in Vogue*. New York: Penguin, 1997. An in-depth study of Harlem and the major figures and events of the Harlem Renaissance that captures the excitement and cultural richness of the period. Includes extensive notes, some black-and-white photographs, and an informative introduction.

David Leverling Lewis, ed., *The Harlem Renaissance Reader*. New York: Viking, 1994. This collection includes work by forty-five figures of the Harlem Renaissance, including previously unpublished material. Although the works are not dated and do not include original publication information, the collection is still very useful. Also includes a strong historical introduction and biographical notes on the major figures of the period.

Alain Locke, ed., *The New Negro: An Interpretation*. New York: Albert and Charles Boni, 1925. This landmark collection of poetry, fiction, drama, and essays by Harlem Renaissance figures is the anthologized version of the *Survey Graphic* issue featuring black culture, literature, and art. Includes several bibliographies, including a list of contributors and lists of works featuring blacks in literature, music, drama, and folklore.

Arnold Rampersad, ed., *The Collected Works of Langston Hughes*. Vol. 1: *The Poems, 1921–1940*. Columbia: University of Missouri Press, 2001. Contains many of Hughes's most celebrated works; also includes a biographical introduction and a chronology of Hughe's life and career.

Studio Museum in Harlem, *Harlem Renaissance Art of Black America*. New York: Abradale, 1987. This book features numerous color and black-and-white photos of art, artists, and sites of the Harlem Renaissance and includes several essays on the period by contemporary scholars. Also includes a chronology of the Harlem Renaissance, a biographical chronology of the artists, and a bibliography of books and magazines illustrated by Aaron Douglas.

Wallace Thurman, *The Blacker the Berry*. New York: Scribner Paperback Fiction, 1996. Thurman's novel (originally published in 1929) explores the conflicts and destructiveness of racial bias in America through its main character, Emma Lou Brown, a dark-skinned girl raised in a light-skinned family who leaves Idaho for the black mecca of Harlem.

Bruce M. Tyler, *From Harlem to Hollywood: The Struggle for Racial and Cultural Democracy, 1920–1943*. New York: Garland, 1992. Each chapter details a facet of African American history and experience as it relates to the arts between 1920 and 1943, including black involvement in the military USO and Hollywood.

Theodore G. Vincent, ed., *Voices of a Black Nation.* San Francisco: Ramparts, 1973. A collection of writings by figures important to the Harlem Renaissance and the New Negro political movement. Each essay is dated and annotated with its original source and publication date, arranged by subject or issue with an introduction by the editor. Includes an appendix listing black American news agencies, magazines, and publishers from World War I to the 1930s.

Steven Watson, *The Harlem Renaissance: Hub of African-American Culture, 1920–1930.* New York: Pantheon, 1995. An illustrated and annotated history of the Harlem Renaissance that covers the major figures and events. Also includes a chronology, extensive notes, lists, and other interesting information and trivia.

Sondra Kathryn Wilson, ed., *The* Crisis *Reader: Stories, Poetry, and Essays from the N.A.A.C.P.'s* Crisis *Magazine.* New York: Modern Library, 1999. A collection of work published in the *Crisis* from the 1910s to the 1930s, featuring the major figures of the Harlem Renaissance. Includes several articles on topics relevant to the period and publication as well as thumbnail biographies of the contributors.

Cary D. Wintz, *Black Culture and the Harlem Renaissance.* Houston: Rice University Press, 1988. Wintz explores the literature of the Harlem Renaissance and how it related to the Harlem community and the political and social events of the period leading up to, during, and after the Renaissance.

Periodicals

Langston Hughes, "The Negro Artist and the Racial Mountain," *Nation*, June 23, 1926.

Videos

The Rise and Fall of Jim Crow. Quest Productions, VideoLine Productions, and Thirteen/WNET New York, 2002. This video series details the history of the so-called Jim Crow laws that legalized segregation and discrimination against nonwhites and the efforts to change and abolish these laws. Includes numerous interviews and historical photographs and footage.

Internet Sources

"Jessie Redmon Fauset," The Black Renaissance in Washington, D.C., 1920–1930s, June 20, 2003. www.dclibrary.org/blkren/bios/fausetjr.html.

Paul P. Reuben, "Chapter 9: Harlem Renaissance, 1919–1937," Perspectives in American Literature, 2004. www.csustan.edu/english/reuben/pal/chap9/chap9.html.

Index

Picture Credits

Cover, © John Springer Collection/CORBIS
© Lucien Aigner/CORBIS, 87
© Bettmann/CORBIS, 8, 11, 14, 18, 22, 25, 28, 35, 42(right), 46, 63, 67, 70, 84, 88, 92, 94
© CORBIS, 31, 38, 41, 42(left, 47, 51
© E.O. Hoppe/CORBIS, 60
Hulton Archive by Getty Images, 17, 65, 71, 73
Courtesy of The Kennedy Center, 54, 55
Library of Congress, 3, 6, 12, 13, 15, 30, 44, 62, 79, 95
Time-Life Pictures/Getty Images, 45, 74
Courtesy of Transylvania University, 36

About the Author

Andy Koopmans is the author of over a dozen books. He lives in Seattle, Washington, with his wife, Angela Mihm, and their pets, Zachary, Bubz, and Licorice. He wishes to thank the staff of Lucent Books, particularly Stuart Miller, for their assistance in preparing this manuscript for publication.